Also by Sofia Samatar

Opacities: On Writing and the Writing Life
The Practice, the Horizon, and the Chain
Tone (with Kate Zambreno)
The White Mosque: A Memoir
Monster Portraits (with Del Samatar)
Tender: Stories
The Winged Histories
A Stranger in Olondria

Friendly City
a year of walks

Sofia Samatar

QUINX BOOKS

Friendly City: A Year of Walks
Copyright © 2025 by Sofia Samatar
All rights reserved.
Quinx Books

Contents

Preface   3

January   5
The Romance of Distance   6
What Is a City?   9
The Cozy Outdoors   13
These Little Touches   17
Things Can Be Small and Still Retain Their Nature   21

February   27
The Wood Between the Worlds   28
Forest Bathing   31
The Inventory of the Streets   35
Frozen Children   39

March   43
The Porous Surface   44
In the Margin of the Margin   49
Natural Light   53
Roses, Roots, Branches, Buds   57

April   63
Looping   64
Bookends   68
University Walks   72
Redbud   76

May 81
Things Have More to Tell 82
Transient Feeling 86
A Dead Sweet Perfume 90
In Deep Time 94
The Language of the Flowers 98

June 103
Work in Progress 104
The Musical City 108
Dappled Things 112
Night Walks 115

July 121
Softness 122
The Smallest House 126
Developments 130
Sites of Memory 134
Animal Encounters 138

August 143
Dear Neighbor 144
Enchanted Forest 147
This Path Is Not for You 151
Why Here? 155

September   161
Everyday Losses   162
Second Spring   166
The Other Side   170
Desire Paths   174

October   179
The Shadowy Street   180
An Attempt at Exhausting Court Square   184
The Voice of the City   192
Ordinary Miracles   196
The Ghost of Evelyn Byrd   200

November   205
Murmuration   206
Small Fates   210
The Image of the City   214
Pedestrian Secrets   218

December   225
Non-Places   226
Street Haunting   231
Salvage   235
The Romance of Closeness   239

FRIENDLY CITY

Preface

In 2016, I moved to Harrisonburg, Virginia, a town known locally by the nickname "the Friendly City." I am a walker, and after seven years of taking long walks in this place—especially during the COVID-19 pandemic—I felt the urge to write about this everyday experience, which seemed to me both simple and mysterious. I proposed a column on walking to Andrew Jenner, founder of *The Harrisonburg Citizen*, an independent online news source. For this project, I walked and wrote every week for one calendar year.

My observations on a year of walking, lightly revised, are collected in this book. Originally, each piece was accompanied by the following heading:

"The Friendly City" is a weekly column about walking in Harrisonburg that will run during 2024. Each week, your friendly correspondent, writer and teacher Sofia Samatar, will reflect on a walk in our city.

January

The Romance of Distance

Anyone can write about a large city—large cities are open to everyone—but small cities can only be portrayed by people who love them.

For the first outing of the year, choose your favorite walk, on a brilliant January day, the streets flooded with white-gold light. Go up one of those shaggy gravel alleys, among the backyards, where the city reveals its most modest and intimate side. How fantastic it is to walk here, among the clotheslines and leaning ladders, the cheerful disarray of overturned pots and jumbles of plastic containers! There's a homey feel to the sheds, some painted red to look like miniature barns, others overgrown with bristling ivy. An ear of dried corn hangs on a fence for birds and squirrels to pick at. Wind chimes ring on the eaves. Swing sets and trampolines creak in the cold. Sunlight gilds everything, raising a fuzzy glow from a rough old tree and a gleam from a motorcycle parked on the grass. Then a cloud drifts across the sun, the chill deepens, you button your coat, but soon you're warm again, because you're walking uphill. For this is a hilly city, a patchwork of dips and rises, where you never have to go far to see the mountains.

This is how you should enjoy your first walk. Maybe it's an afternoon walk, because you've waited until the warmest part of the day. Someone's been trimming a pine tree; feathery branches lie in the yard. You breathe the clean evergreen scent and the richer brown smell of moldering leaves. There aren't many people around at this hour—the children are still at school, the adults at work—but you, you're walking, it's the time when convalescents go out, the hour of people who march on the doctor's orders, of university professors fortunate enough to enjoy a long vacation, of retired people, of unemployed people, of artists, of pastors who discover a free afternoon, of people who work from home and can slip out when no one else is around. But where are all these imagined walkers? You come across no one but a man washing a van, who greets you with a wave in accordance with the culture of the city. You nod and return the gesture. At the corner, you pass a small memorial: a wooden cross nailed to a telephone pole, adorned with pink fabric roses.

A dog starts barking at you, and then all the dogs join in, their hoarse cries strung from yard to yard. They fade as you enter a silent neighborhood, one that seems new, the trees still small, the houses formidably tidy, all neat brick and spotless siding. You're going uphill again, and it's just quiet, there's nothing happening, and you feel as if nothing ever happens here, and you realize that of course the Friendly City, like any place on earth, will be different for different people. There will be people who find this stillness dull, perhaps unbearable, who long for the action and romance of urban centers, and others whose experiences have taught them to treasure this silence, who cling to the hush of this town where you can hear the trees stirring in the breeze. For these, there may be solace in the bare branches with the birds' nests exposed, the empty lawns in their drab winter yellow, the houses that all seem to have their eyes shut, the faint sound of traffic from Highway 42, and farther off, almost imperceptible, the monotonous buzz of a saw.

At the top of the hill, a vista opens. Suddenly you're above the trees, face to face with the indigo ridge of Massanutten. You think of Novalis, the eighteenth-century German Romantic poet, who identified distance with poetry. Everything becomes poetic with distance, Novalis said: mountains, people, philosophies, events. A shift in perspective transforms everything. For Novalis, this was no cheap illusion, but a key to the deepest level of human experience. And even though you know there's nothing very romantic down below—gas stations, a livestock auction, a poultry plant—you're enchanted by this glimpse through a magic mirror that makes the earth recede and enlarges the sky to a swath of watered silk. The landscape has changed, the trees crouching like children playing at hide-and-seek, the mountains surging proudly across the horizon. And it occurs to you that if the Friendly City has romance, it's right here, in this ordinary and profound effect of geography: the opportunity to encounter, if just for a moment, a dramatically altered view of the world, merely by walking uphill.

What Is a City?

ON A MORNING OF FOG, the trees gray with frost after the ice storm, I'm wondering: What is a city?

Only the houses directly in front of me stand out clearly. The trees behind them are thin ghosts, seeping into the vapor of the sky. A string of lights, left behind by the holiday season, picks out the shape of a porch railing down the street, twinkling in the dense mist.

With so little visibility, you could imagine yourself in the country, especially when passing a wonderful old peeling house, its windows blind, its walls darkened by somber bushes, that seems to stand all alone in the street, isolated by the fog.

As I walk downhill, the mist lifts. A clicking fills the air: icicles dropping from telephone wires. Since the sidewalk is icy, I stroll in the street, and this is part of what makes the Friendly City feel like a small town to me, not like a city at all. How easy it is to step out into the street, carefully of course, staying close to the parked cars, but without a real sense of danger, confident that any passing vehicle will move at a decorous speed, giving me time to retreat, and anyway, there won't be too many of them.

I think of the *New York Times* opinion piece a friend sent me recently, "Baudelaire Would Be Run Over in New

York City Today," in which the writer Shaan Sachdev laments a lost New York where he used to wander in a reverie like the iconic flaneur, the city walker described by the poet Charles Baudelaire. For a flaneur, urban walks are adventures, dreams, and invitations to philosophy. Walking is a particularly loose and creative form of thinking. Sachdev worries about what will happen to ideas when walking becomes too hazardous to allow for contemplation. Last summer, he was hit by three bikes.

As the sun melts the ice, each tree releases a private rain. I'm still walking in the street, not because the sidewalk is slick but because there's no sidewalk—a common occurrence in the Friendly City, for our sidewalk is an unpredictable animal with a lively sense of humor. It bounds up, smooth and amiable underfoot, then dives out of sight, leaving the unsuspecting walker stranded on a neighbor's grass. There it is again, coaxing you uphill with the promise of a pleasant ramble; then it dumps you unceremoniously in the street. A friend once told me that early in the city's history, homeowners were given the choice whether or not to permit a sidewalk in front of their houses, a form of city planning that strikes me as frankly deranged, but would explain why our sidewalk sometimes pops up, wagging its tail, for the length of a single property. In the Friendly City, you must always be prepared to arrive at that magical, tricky place immortalized in Shel Silverstein's children's book *Where the Sidewalk Ends*. This scruffy, half-grown, misbehaving sidewalk gives our city a small-town air, the feeling of a place that has not yet fully arrived.

Cross the railroad track. Cut through the garden of Liberty Park, its trees dripping crystal. Behind the park, a wooden bridge spans the creek. Today the planks are treacherous with slush, and I slide along cautiously, peering down into the shallow slate-gray water. When you walk in the Friendly City, you often pass these twin conduits, the railroad track and the creek, and I think this intensifies the small-town atmosphere, the feeling that this is a minor place, where the train doesn't stop, where everything passes through—the water, the boxcars, and, when you reach downtown, the huge trucks that fill the streets with their thunder, dwarfing the shops and restaurants, as if this place were merely a stretch of highway.

On the courthouse lawn, a plaque informs me that the town was founded in 1779 and became a city in 1916. I'm sure this urban status has to do with population density, and that, technically, this place qualifies as a city. But in the collective imagination, a city is more than an official population threshold. It's energy, risk, opportunity, and above all crowds, those crowds in which, according to Baudelaire, the flaneur should swim like a fish in water, and you won't find crowds like that in the Friendly City, especially not on a Sunday after an ice storm, unless it's the flock of ducks sunning themselves on the bank of the creek. Honestly, I don't think Baudelaire could stand this town. If you asked him, "Charles, would you rather live without crowds or get hit by a bike?" I think he'd say, "Donnez-moi le vélo."* But if Sachdev is right, and the act of wandering is intimately tied to the act of wondering,

---

* "Give me the bike."

then it's worth noting that it's still possible to wander here, ambling along the streets, stepping off the curb where the sidewalk ends, falling into daydreams, your gaze sliding down the gentle curve of Main Street, catching for a moment on the red of the pawnshop sign, then slipping free, drawn out like the train, like the waters of the creek, your thoughts bubbling through the air with the rhythm of your strides.

What is this feeling of secrecy, this delight? Even in vivid winter sunlight, the Friendly City seems a little bit veiled, as if still wrapped in fog: the protective cloak of its power to go unnoticed, to be just another place along the road.

The Cozy Outdoors

For the past few years, winter in the Friendly City has been mild, the holiday season almost balmy. How enchanting, then, to wake and find the street transformed into one of those blue globes enclosing a snowy scene!

Cobalt clouds thicken the sky, reflected in the blue pallor of the snow. The very air seems blue. The parked cars are draped in winter shawls, pale blue like skimmed milk. There isn't enough snow to cover the street, which carves a dark line between the silvery ranks of the porches. But in the Friendly City, we're not greedy—nor are we prepared to deal with severe weather events. Extravagance doesn't suit us. We like unpretentious shops, serviceable vehicles, sensible shoes, and nice, considerate snowfalls that know their place.

At ten o'clock, a fine snow is still falling. Paw prints speckle the whiteness covering my porch steps. When I open the door, the neighbor's cat runs up to meet me, crying to get into my house, where I know from experience he will make himself right at home. From his prints in the snow, I can see he's been going from door to door, this bold striped animal, a most civic-minded member of our community, always confident of a welcome and ready to repay generous neighbors by purring and rubbing his bulk against their calves. In this cat's opinion, all doors should stand open and all who seek lodging should find it. I wish I could practice this radical ideal. But I don't want to leave him alone in my house, so I click my tongue at him, half scolding, half apologizing, until he pads off to the next door.

The snow is not deep—perhaps an inch has fallen. The blue note has faded from the air, leaving behind a charcoal sketch: a dark gray street, a pale gray sky, and snow trampled into grayish slush or lying thin on the lawns, grass poking through like pencil strokes. Overhead, a turkey vulture moves lazily, gliding across cloud cover that seems stretched just above the treetops, a sky pegged down like stiff, resistant fabric. It's a tweed sky, an upholstered sky, what I think of as a Dutch sky, after the paintings of the Old Masters: heavy, dirty-looking, tinged with yellow, giving the town a closed-in feeling, shutting out the wind.

On a day of snow, the outdoors immediately suggests the indoors. Falling snow means canceled school, postponed meetings, and a desire for hibernation, especially in the Friendly City, where we take even a small amount of snow very seriously. A snowplow lumbers past, rolling down a street where not a single flake has stuck. I'm not sure what it will find to plow, but I admire the industry. This vigilant snowplow flashes an orange light against the windows, advising caution, hot chocolate, and, if possible, pajamas all day.

But, as I suspected, the children are out. Approaching the elementary school, I see a grownup struggling across the snowy grass, dragging a sled with two little ones aboard, one in a bright lavender coat, the other in turquoise. And on the slope behind the school, they're sledding. They're marching uphill with their candy-colored sleds, then sliding down. There goes a shrieking elf on a plastic disc. Some of them are really flying! Somehow they've scraped together enough snow to build a ramp. Winter sports are being enjoyed here on a small scale, under the fan shapes of the bare trees, the lowering, snow-laden Dutch sky. From a distance, the sledders look like characters out of one of those old paintings, tiny hunters and skaters whose active forms enliven the landscape.

Here come two children clinging to a toboggan, howling in unison. A man whooping with a child on his lap. Does the snow create an indoor feeling? If so, it's not only because it encourages people to stay inside but because it can transform the outside into an intimate space. I think again of those Dutch painters who were famous for their interiors, their domestic scenes, and their small canvases, and how even a picture of a frozen canal, which might be so dreary, takes on a festive air when it's filled with skating figures.

An outdoor feeling, but thoroughly domesticated. This is not a wild outdoors, not a lonely outdoors. It's a cozy outdoors.

The slope is turning darker, the snow mixed with grass and mud, but the sledders still whizz down, their ramp a compact knob. Their cries ring out faintly, as if muffled by the sky that hangs over the city like a curtain dampened by kitchen steam.

As I turn aside to continue my walk, I catch sight of a lone child seated on a sled, slowly maneuvering it across the flat expanse of the playground, leaning back to push against the ground, inching the runners forward: a solitary wanderer traversing an icy swamp.

These Little Touches

EXTREME BRIGHTNESS of January sun. Is it possible to walk off sorrow? Thick ice coats the edges of the streets, drawing the light toward it, playing with it, and throwing it back to the cold blue sky, where a patch of moon is stamped like a thumbprint of chalk. A walk can feel so arbitrary and useless. It's an activity that could easily be skipped, exchanged for something more productive, some practical confrontation with a source of heartache, whether personal, communal, or global.

My stroll is gratuitous, extra, like one of my favorite spots in town, the little bike path I'm entering now: a brief stretch of pavement, laughably short, which takes me about a minute to walk. What is the point of this path? Who decided it was essential for cyclists to cut through this strip of scrub behind the Family Dollar? I imagine a whimsical city planner, or one who'd had too much coffee. To enter the bike path, you pass the mechanic, where people are often working outside, but not today—the cold has driven everyone indoors, and the only sign of life in the mechanic's shop is a trail of smoke seeping up from the roof. Cars sag in the yard among stray tires and children's scooters, all covered with snow. A simple two-railed fence separates the shop from the path, a barrier of rough, greenish wood that suggests you've wandered into a country lane, or even a different era.

This fence reminds me of my morning reading: a newspaper from the Friendly City one hundred years ago. I'd learned from my friend the historian that the city's old papers had been digitized, so I opened an online archive for a glimpse of January 1924. Scanned pages filled my laptop screen, modern in form yet timeworn in quality, the text sometimes blackened into illegibility, the salvaged articles and advertisements rising out of the damaged print like flotsam on a dark stream.

In 1924, I read, the hog market was growing. A local veterinarian issued a plea for dairies to improve sanitation. In Washington, DC, President Coolidge caused a stir by visiting an African American neighborhood to call on the ailing Arthur Brooks, valet to presidents since the Taft administration. Five day-trippers from Staunton narrowly escaped tragedy when their car tumbled into a culvert. Two professors at William and Mary were arrested for duck hunting after dark. A resident of the Friendly City placed a hopeful ad asking for the return of a box of Brown's Mule Tobacco, mislaid downtown on Saturday night.

I'm walking up the bike path, the trees on my left closing off the city, the sound of traffic fading. On my right, the trees have been cut down, and it gives me a pang to remember them, for there was a time when they turned this corner of town into a secret forest. Now that side of the bike path has been torn open, revealing rectangular rows of storage units with green metal doors. Cars pass on the road beyond. There's no longer a sense of being secluded from the world for the length of a breath. Gone are the thickets where I used to see deer, where tents were pitched in the shade. But a row of pines has been planted beside the storage units, so I have hope that something like the old greenwood will come back. And the house at the end of the path, with its little windows and steeply slanted roof, still encourages dreams, making me wonder what it's like to live in this odd, quiet nook, enclosed in this sun-streaked hush.

When I turn and look back along the path, my heart lifts. For an instant, despite the lost trees, I see an enchanted corridor receding into mystery. The city has disappeared. This isn't a bike path, it's not a road, it's *the* road, the one the child takes in the fairy tale, toward adventure.

A fleeting illusion. Inessential, extra. A scrap of ribbon tied to the city.

I leave the path and walk up the street. Here are some items for sale in a yard: gas cans, a tire, a mover's dolly. I think of the 1924 auction I read about this morning, in which two cows and two steers would be sold, along with a hundred chickens, a 1918 Ford Model T touring car, three tons of coal, and a dinner bell. Reading the list, I felt as if I was there, crossing the yard where the Ford stood parked by the woodpile, walking through the house. "Very old library table, in excellent condition; 'secretary' or desk and book-case combined, 100 years old or more; walnut chest, new cedar chest, lot of chairs, rockers, beds, carpets, linoleum . . ." I saw the antique sewing machine, the parlor organ, and the Silvertone phonograph with "a choice lot of records." But I was most moved by the little things, as the list began to trail off, as if the house were running out of ways to prove its worth. "Meat tub, vinegar barrel, canned fruit, empty cans, jellies, preserves, honey, etc. . . . and many other things too numerous to mention."

No, it's not possible to walk off sorrow. Your walk is not a cure. It's just one of the ten thousand things.

I pass a yard where a pinwheel casts a spinning shadow on the snow. Farther on, a terracotta figure prays inside a shell. There's a mirror propped on a porch to catch the light. A plaster gargoyle. So many plant pots. These little touches. A green glass bird.

Things Can Be Small and Still Retain Their Nature

Today I'm thinking about the authenticity of little things.

Walk across town, westward toward the Alleghenies, on a springlike winter day, the snow all melted, the wind smelling of the thaw, the sky a medley of blue and gray with distinct, finely drawn clouds above the mountains. How serene these clouds look, like floating islands, dark on the bottom, shimmering white on top, repeating the shape of the mountains as the mountains repeat the color of the sky. It's as if the sky and the mountains have been rendered with the same paint, but on the mountains the stuff has been laid on more thickly, perhaps with a palette knife: the work of a frugal artist with a single pigment in the box, a genius of minimalism.

At the end of the road, the wind comes rushing across a stretch of open land, a broad meadow I imagine belongs to the nearby church, the whey-colored grass tipped with azure as if it's inhaled some of the color of the sky. From here I can trace the road with a glance, all the way down the hill, then all the way up on the other side of Market Street, taking in the houses, the trees, the farm-equipment dealership where red and blue tractors stand in rows, and beyond that the forest, the trees rising like smoke: the dim, bosky shadow of Westover Park.

It's a little forest, but it's still a forest. As I walk downhill, I feel it's time for me to accept the Friendly City as a real city. The church on the opposite side of Market Street slides into view, so that I have one church behind me and another in front. And there—yes—beyond the church on Market Street, I spy the steeple of a third church! Pausing just here, if I turn my head, I can see three churches. I remember when our cousins came to visit, flying in from their home in the capital of another country, how amazed they were at our abundance of churches, making up a Spot the Steeple game as they explored the town. "Look, another church!" "Hey, there's another!" I wonder if all these churches can possibly be full on a Sunday morning. And that reminds me of the famous verse "For where two or three are gathered together in my name, there am I in the midst of them."

A compressed philosophy of minor things.

Cross Market Street. There's one of my favorite houses, huddled beneath a stand of towering oaks. How delightful to see a little house surrounded by big trees! It looks as if it's snuggling against their trunks. With its low, shady porch, it has the charm of a hobbit house, a burrow, a place to curl up and drowse through the winter.

A mechanical droning reaches me from the auto repair shop on Market Street. In the Friendly City, you're always running up against something mini-industrial, alongside something mini-rural, mini-wild, or mini-urban. And each fragment is fully itself.

Across Dogwood Street, I step onto a grassy slope with the delicious name of Green Angel Park. The creek, Blacks Run, flows along the bottom. There's a little wooden bridge where I stop to look down at the water, which gleams like ink as the daylight starts to fade. Trees crowd the banks, and tufts of long, yellowish reeds cushion its edges, so it looks soft, a creek bed that's really a bed, the water nestling there, just on the verge of sleep, murmuring gently to itself among the stones.

My bridge spans the water, taking me safely from bank to bank. And although I might be able to jump the creek with a good running start, my bridge is still a bridge. Oh, happy bridge, little toy bridge! I want to take a piece of it home, a splinter.

On my way back, I pass a yard that's completely overgrown, rampant among the neighboring clipped lawns. This bushy yard, with its profusion of dry weeds and brown winter branches, creates a dark, rustling pocket in the curve of the street. It might feel sinister if it wasn't so small you can see right through it to the porch. In the tangled ivy, a crooked sign reads Wildlife Sanctuary. There's something comical about it—isn't this wee jungle claiming too much? What kind of wildlife is taking refuge here, other than squirrels and spiders? But then again, aren't those creatures legitimately wild, even if pint-sized? And surely this yard might attract other beings to its cover—shy groundhogs, warblers in search of insects, an exhausted possum fleeing the terror of the traffic.

Maybe this sign is a joke, like a grin toward neighbors who might frown at this rambling yard. Or maybe it means to say seriously: *Here is the dark wood.* Through the knotty branches, I glimpse an inscrutable line of standing stones: a miniature Stonehenge awaiting a visit from Lilliputian druids.

February

The Wood Between the Worlds

IF YOU CROSS THE BRIDGE at Green Angel Park and climb the hill, you will enter the Wood Between the Worlds.

Such silence. The street sounds dwindle as you ascend. Market Street runs below, forming the border of the wood. Peering down there, you can see cars passing, the glint of the grocery store. But you are under these trees.

In *The Magician's Nephew* by C. S. Lewis, two children enter an enchanted wood. They call it the Wood Between the Worlds because it's an in-between place, a portal to a variety of worlds, including our own. "It was the quietest wood you could possibly imagine," Lewis writes. "There were no birds, no insects, no animals, and no wind." The wood is a sort of limbo, with no action and no real character. Yet it's deeply alive. "You could almost feel the trees growing."

I call this slope at Westover Park the Wood Between the Worlds for these qualities: stillness, silence, and symmetry.

Like the magical transit zone in the children's story, our wood is made up of straight trunks and level, manicured grass. It's not a wild place by any means. The ground is clear, the trees identical tall evergreens, evenly planted like pillars in some fantastical piece of architecture, their shadows recalling the striped walls of the palace of the Alhambra in Spain, and perhaps this is what creates such a strong impression of silence: the sense that one is inside some vast hall. For the wood is not really soundless. Under the trees I can hear the traffic, small birds twittering—including my favorite, the rapturously musical cardinal—and a small plane going by overhead, maybe one of the ones our cousin flew when he worked for the nearby aircraft company, and then, far off but clear in the chilly February air, the lonely lamentation of the train.

The note of the train is the most mournful sound! How it floats across the city, bearing its insistent message of farewell. I love that the train goes through the Friendly City, even if I can't have my dream of a local passenger stop. The call of the train is a childhood sound for me, because even though I moved often as a child, I never lived far from a railroad track. In the little towns where I grew up, the little town where I used to go to visit my aunt, the little town where I live now—in all of these places you can hear the train. That grieving, fading whistle suggests continuity even as it announces departure. It gives rise to the startling thought that I've never moved at all, that the little towns where I've lived are all the same town, a place where the air is shaped by these sound waves, imprinted with this passing cry.

In its effect on the imagination, the sound of the train is a portal to other places and times: an auditory Wood Between the Worlds.

Before I came to the Friendly City, I had never lived anywhere for more than five years in a row. But I've just completed my seventh year in this town. Seven years! A magic number. In writing these notes, I invoke the spirit of these streets where I've lived longer than anywhere else. Celebrating a place, I'm also celebrating time.

In the Wood Between the Worlds, there is no time. Life gathers, richly abundant, but doesn't move. There is no change. Or perhaps it only appears that way to the children in the story. Who are we to tell the time of trees?

At the top of the ridge, by the chain-link fence, I peep over a steep slope crackling with vegetation—the undisciplined forest on the other side of the park. I remember the first time I walked here, how exciting it was to feel like I was hiking. Yes, there's a piece of the forest in the middle of the city! A few steps carry me into resin-scented air. For as long as I'm here, I'll embrace the zone where the urban meets the wilderness: the Friendly City, my Wood Between the Worlds.

Forest Bathing

Do you know the entrance to the forest?

I don't mean the Wood Between the Worlds, with its regimented, formal lines, the parking lot showing between the trunks. I mean the real forest. At the top of Westover Park, where the fence ends, a gap opens in the trees and you can go down a trail into a gnarled, secluded wood.

A sudden chill—it's always a few degrees cooler under this canopy. The trail descends steeply among the gray trunks, the bright needles of young pines. A carpet of fallen leaves covers the ground, sending up a delicate, smoky scent.

In his book *Forest Bathing: How Trees Can Help You Find Health and Happiness*, Dr. Qing Li writes of the Japanese practice of *shinrin-yoku*, or forest bathing: taking in the atmosphere of the forest. Dr. Li, who directs the Forest Therapy Society in Japan, is quick to point out that forest bathing is different from hiking or jogging. You don't have to move at all. The idea is to draw in the forest through all your senses. He recommends listening to the breeze in the leaves, watching the light through the branches, breathing in the natural aromatherapy of the air, tasting it on your tongue, placing your hands on the trees, and lying on the ground. His book is packed with data showing how *shinrin-yoku* can improve your odds against a host of ills, from anxiety to cancer. I'm charmed by his authoritative tone. "Drink in the flavor of the forest," he commands, adding confidently: "Now you have connected with nature. You have crossed the bridge to happiness."

As for me, I've crossed the bike path and plunged into the forest on the far side. I step over roots and rocks, clamber across a log. The trees grow thicker, the shadows denser. Huge stones lie tumbled in a gorge. I observe the mossy boulders, the oaks that have shaded them for long years. I breathe the powdery air of the winter forest, savor its sweet bark taste. Listen to the oddly mechanical squawk of a squirrel. Pull off my glove, brush my fingers over a fall of ivy. Fully immersed: forest bathing.

How lucky we are, in this little city, to be able to soak in this deep, verdant reservoir!

Walking back up the trail toward the park, I reflect with pleasure on the beneficial plant chemicals filling the air, which according to Dr. Li are now lowering my stress hormones, boosting my anticancer proteins, and predisposing me toward a good night's sleep. I'm considering scraping my fingers through the soil to pick up some *Mycobacterium vaccae*, a boon for the immune system, when I realize the path before me looks odd and unfamiliar, the trees looming too close. I've taken the wrong trail.

With a laugh, I retrace my steps. There are several trails in this wood, crisscrossing each other, but I'm not worried—I just have to find one that leads uphill. I remember how the path rose along the gorge. The bareness of the February trees should make it easy to spot the way out.

It's not this way, though. No.

The trail has changed. It's wider, flatter. This is not the way I came in.

Birds chitter. The squirrel's chuckle takes on a jeering note.

Go back. Try another path. Stripes of light. Dry leaves underfoot. Trees. More trees.

A maze of trails. Forest bathing? I'm forest drowning.

Friends and neighbors, I assure you that you can get lost in the woods in the middle of our city.

Help! I'm walking faster, unbuttoning my coat in a flush of nerves. There's no one around. Then the trees grow thinner. Relief—escape—a gap! But this outlet leads straight into somebody's yard. Do I dash across the lawn? The street is so near, just a few yards away!

How far does the friendliness of the Friendly City go? I don't think it extends to letting strangers run through your yard. I remember our next-door neighbor—an elderly woman who lived alone, with whom we got along very well until her death a few years ago—who kept two loaded shotguns behind her door. I wonder if I can be identified from a window as a person of color, and if this should make me even more worried. But what keeps me out of this yard is not an analysis of race relations or gun violence. It's my sense of propriety. I'm held back by a polite reserve, an instinctive bashfulness—an absurd feeling, but one that's in tune with the quiet neighborhood on the other side of the trees.

Back into the forest. Oh! There's a sign that reads Private Property: No Trespassing. I'm as embarrassed as if I've walked in on somebody on the toilet. Excuse me, forgive me! I rush up the trail. Enormous gray stones line the route, grinning at me like the very teeth of the earth.

Suddenly, there's a gate: an iron gate in the middle of the path, all on its own, with no fence attached, standing open.

The eeriness of this gate all alone in the wood! If I go through, I'm sure I'll be put to work as the Fairy Queen's handmaiden for a hundred years. I'll have to polish her beetle-wing shoes and take care of her sickly, squalling, pointy-eared baby. When I return to the world of mortals, everyone I know will be dead.

I back away from this eldritch door. And at last, as you have guessed, dear neighbors, I find my way out and write these words to you. I bring you news of the wildwood in the city, a dusky labyrinth offering all the elements, both material and imaginary, evoked by the word *forest*. Here you can practice *shinrin-yoku*, absorbing the leaf-rich air in an act as old as our species, which is also a modern therapy. Here you can lose your way. You can feel vulnerable, bewildered, thrilled, renewed. You can test and analyze your character. You might even be stolen by the fairies. It's the expansive atmosphere of the forest, rather than what happens there, that constitutes the bridge to happiness.

The Inventory of the Streets

A BLUSTERY DAY, blue and silver and black and white. A sky of smoke and metal, constantly in motion, the clouds dark as charcoal in the center but ringed with a blazing platinum glow. The strong gusts give an impression of industry, as if the sky has been turned into a workshop. It's the sort of day that would have been represented in old pictures by the image of Zephyr, the wind god, blowing vigorously, his cheeks swollen with the effort. A day for walking up Third Street to Washington, into a zone of enterprise: the busy, semi-industrial edge of the city.

I cross Liberty Street and head downhill between the factories that represent the venerable poultry-raising tradition in this valley. On one side, there's the Farmer Focus mural, a silhouette of a man and a boy in broad-brimmed hats, walking hand in hand with a few chickens at their feet. On the other side, the grain elevator rises, one of the city's tallest structures and a convenient landmark for me, as my house lies almost in its shadow. At home, we call it the Tower of Mordor—a nickname I thought was only used by our family until I met another resident of the Friendly City who referred to it as Minas Morgul, provoking the suspicion that the whole city dreams a red eye watches them from the heights of this edifice.

Picking my way across the railroad tracks, which expand to a double line in this part of town, I nod apologetically to passing drivers, who look surprised to encounter a human being among the parking lots and commercial buildings. It's midday, the wrong hour for people. In general, walkers appear here only before dawn and after dusk, when the workers tramp to and from their shifts in their gumboots and hairnets. For most of the day, in the environs of the city's largest business concerns, where so much activity is concentrated, so many human and animal bodies in motion, a walker can get the feeling that the place is entirely deserted, and that she, as a living being, doesn't belong here, and had better pick up her pace.

There's a different feeling at the bottom of the hill, among the small auto repair shops. The neighborhood has a bustling quality, business and residential activities so mixed that many of the businesses have taken up residence in the houses. Among the homes converted into shops where mechanics ply their trade, my eye jumps dizzily from slender porch posts to the gleam of a pile of hubcaps, from the baroque scrollwork of gingerbread trim to a crowd of wrecked cars with yawning hoods. There's a lively air to this jumble of colors, materials, and styles. Here's a white picket fence, then the garden of the local environmental nonprofit, then a sign for Windshield City, then a tiny house standing alone on a plain of gravel where a diminutive dog barks plaintively. From a porch built low and close to the street, almost on the sidewalk, a wooden rocking horse observes some mechanics discussing a broken-down camper. A Thanksgiving wreath in faded fall colors hangs over a stack of steering wheels. And the bright blue wall of a house advertising snow removal and lawn service, saturated with color, rises from its surroundings with the bold effect of an abstract painting.

"The inventory of the streets is inexhaustible," the German writer Walter Benjamin observed in his *Moscow Diary*, written when he visited that metropolis in 1926. How startling to realize that the same is true of the streets of this little city, which offer endless material for contemplation. You only have to begin to pay attention in order to open a treasure trove of sights inviting reverie. Circling back toward my house, I feel drawn into the vibrancy of these small establishments that have sprung up between the big ones like weeds through the cracks in a sidewalk, heartened by the sight of people at work in full view, where they can make eye contact and wave at a stranger, and also aware of their precarity, the steep odds against their success, as I pass the place where my car received excellent service last year and find it closed down, the sign erased, the lot surrounded with yellow tape. Behind dirty glass, two black swivel chairs hold court in the empty office. It's hard here, hard and unfriendly, I think, returning uphill. Or maybe it would be more accurate to call the city a crazy quilt, a ragbag of colors and textures, feats and failures, energies and ghosts.

An urn in a yard. Two tree trunks with all the branches lopped off. At the top of the hill, a sweeping view toward the big blue shoulder of the mountain. No one appears to be enjoying this prospect today but the garden statues on a nearby lawn, a menagerie of fabricated beasts. A sad terracotta dog. A pink plastic deer with a calm gaze. A bear holding a plant pot. A pair of plaster ducks eaten away by the rain. Such a strange crossroads: manufactured animals standing sentinel over the halls where real animals are processed. A silent commentary on the transformation of matter, living things into dead ones that feed the living, inert materials into the semblance of live creatures. At the edge of the yard, a green gnome spattered with white paint raises an arm with a flourish, as if to say, *See!*

A cardboard box lies in the street; I drag it to the curb. Under some scraggy trees, a vine grows rampantly, twining itself around objects no one has bothered to get rid of: plastic bottles, a sunken tire, a box covered with rotting newspaper. In the coils of this voracious vine, crushed soda cans glint like the wreckage of an ancient civilization. And a lost Christmas ornament, a perfect crimson sphere, throws off such a blinding reflection of a shaft of sunlight that for a moment the street appears to be in flames.

Frozen Children

Walk in any direction and you will find them: the frozen children of our town.

A statue of a boy with a tousled mop of hair. He wears a robe and a cap vaguely suggestive of some religious order. He carries a basin before him in both hands, pitched at an angle as if he's about to empty it on the grass.

They are standing on the lawns, on the gravel paths, within the shadows of the eaves.

A shepherdess turned to one side, her dress slipping from her shoulder. Her skin has a greenish hue. Rosettes on her skirt, curls twisted on her forehead, a long braid down her back.

A granite angel squatting in the weeds. Another praying with clasped hands. A third holding up a lantern.

They are watching in the gardens, in their charmed stillness, their unshakable poise. Silence flows out of them.

A boy with a sullen face, tangled stone locks on his brow, bears a basket of dried petals.

A pair seated on a bench. They are perhaps six inches tall. The girl, who looks younger, rests her head on the boy's shoulder.

They are handsome, chipped, weather-beaten, gleaming in the rain, in every condition from shop-floor brightness to genteel decay. Many are winged, but they never fly. They wait. They adorn the steps and porches, guard the birdbaths, populate the yards.

A black child with white hair clutches a rabbit in both arms.

A plaster child in full color, almost life-size, lounges on a bench. Brown curly hair, a maroon jacket with a broad sailor collar. His dog beside him, he observes the passing cars.

The question of scale seems not to trouble these children. The boy with the straw hat stands at his ease beside a blue jug twice his size. The large stone girl, her apron spread wide, is content to share the lawn with a pair of minuscule tots who only come up to her knee.

Is this their role: to beckon us toward a world where everyday concerns dissolve?

Are they more than decorative? Do they have some message to impart? A ragged cherub leans against a rusty railing, holding up both hands. Eternal gesture of supplication.

There is a popular statue I have spotted three times around town: a child in a graceful, dancing posture atop an ornate birdbath. The bath or fountain is made of three tiered basins with scalloped edges. The child is a stone angel, or maybe a human child with a ruffled, windblown cloak. Light and airy it stands, motionless yet making an irresistible impression of movement with its wavy hair, its crossed hands and feet, the drapery of its short dress, and the cloak or wings half furled about it—a spirit belonging equally to water and ice.

I have seen one in pale stone, another in bronze coated

with verdigris, and then, in a sunless garden below the level of the street, a third one completely green with moss, so overgrown with vegetation its winsome features could hardly be discerned.

I'm reminded of the Lares, the household gods of ancient Rome. These protective spirits were often represented as lively youths. They wore short tunics, flared in winglike folds. Ringlets or wreaths clustered on their brows. They held the sacred vessels, the drinking horn and the offering dish.

A painted angel, her black, flowing tresses crowned with pink roses, her hands cupped. A dark metal girl in the shadow of a fence, head bowed, skirt held out as if to catch a harvest of berries. How often the frozen children seem ready to hold something for us! Their stretched skirts, hollowed palms, basins, and baskets—are they just pretty receptacles for rain and snow? I have read that the Lares shrank over time, fading into folklore, becoming the brownies of nursery tales, who perform household chores if given a bowl of cream. Are they also watching over our yards?

The Lares belonged to individual homes but also to roads, neighborhoods, and cities. These frozen children outside the public library, then, may represent the spirit of this place. Summer and winter they keep their vigil, back to back, the girl perched on a stack of volumes, the boy standing upright. At five o'clock, when the streets begin to empty, these local guardians diffuse an air of green and golden peace. In place of the ritual bowls from which the Romans poured libations long ago, they are holding open books.

March

The Porous Surface

IN THE FRIENDLY CITY, March has many moods. It's not just that it comes in like a lion and goes out like a lamb; March is a riot of textures, featuring extremes of hardness and softness that seem unrelated, as if they're happening not at different times but in different countries. There are bright, pale, golden days, when the atmosphere is as flat and clean as a plate-glass window, and days as cottony and gray as a cat's fur, when the budding trees are bandaged in the damp wool batting of the sky.

Today is one of those soft, drizzly days. I'm still wearing gloves against the chill, but daffodils trumpet from the yards: these gilded bugles, the heralds of spring, their color so intense it seems to ring out. Underneath them, peeping up in their bright yellow, striped, and purple gowns, the crocuses add their children's chorus. I am going down to Blacks Run, a stretch of water that twists and tunnels through the city, making its way to Cooks Creek, the North River, and eventually the Chesapeake Bay.

Blacks Run is a creek with grit, both metaphorical and literal: It's tenacious and dirty. Peering over the bridge at Rock Street, I watch the low, lead-gray water flowing over the stones, coiling around clumps of grass, Styrofoam cups, and plastic bags. Local legend holds that the name Blacks Run has its origin in filth, since the water ran dark in the days of the tannery that used to stand downtown, dumping tannins and other chemicals into the stream. In the 1990s, sewage was still being piped straight into Blacks Run. In 1996, the Virginia Department of Environmental Quality declared the creek impaired. Since then, restoration efforts and a community cleanup campaign have made some improvements, rendering the water attractive to ducks and even a few fish.

The creek hasn't fully healed. It's still impaired, sickened by fertilizers and waste, but the ducks flock to it. As I walk along its edge, a huge drake flies up from under the bridge, then touches down on the water, its jeweled head upraised. I usually think of a drake's head as its most dramatic feature, but today I'm dazzled by its pure white throat, like a beacon between the green head and brown back, in this corridor of drab water and leafless trees. To follow the creek, I walk through a parking lot behind an apartment building, where more ducks squat placidly on the pavement. Soon their families will be stopping traffic on Liberty Street, where a line of sluggish cars, creeping forward by inches and honking their horns, is a sure sign of spring.

Dumpsters. Trash spilling into the creek: bottles and forks, chip bags, an old pair of jeans. Then, at Liberty Park, a rain garden on the bank, where a signboard explains how the garden filters water before it seeps into the ground, reducing pollution and erosion. "This mimics the natural system in an area before it is developed with impervious surfaces such as sidewalks, parking lots, and roofs." Most of the time, I walk on impervious surfaces, but today I'm trying to follow the porous surface. What could embody this quality more fully than the creek, so open and responsive it forms a circle of ripples for each drop of rain?

Blacks Run ducks under the street, so I cross to find it on the other side; then suddenly it disappears beneath the tarmac, popping up on the opposite side, so I cross again. The creek dances with the street, making a pattern of hardness and softness like March weather. Now it wriggles under the old seed company building, its progress hampered by broken bricks and bags of garbage, aluminum cans glinting where it disappears in the dark. I think of the annual Blacks Run Clean-Up Day, when volunteers collect tons of refuse from the stream. The project's website informs me that lots of tires are thrown into the creek. Twenty-five tires were extracted in 2019, while in 2021 the haul included thirteen tires and a hair salon hairdryer.

Friends and neighbors, I ask you—who throws a whole salon hairdryer into a creek? Was it a prank? Sabotage by a rival hairdresser? An outburst of cosmetological rage? Musing on this, I notice I've lost Blacks Run and am now walking along the railroad track without a creek in sight. I round the corner, glimpsing the courthouse clock tower with its sea-green roof, the statue of Justice lifting her scales in the rain, and the replica of the domed springhouse that once marked the spot where fresh water welled out of the ground: the original source of the city.

I have read that they used to call it Big Spring and Never

-Failing Spring. When the replica of the old gazebo was put up in 1995, a sign warned residents not to drink the water. Now I can't even find the path of that water, just the red neon sign of the bail bond agent and several parked police cars. Can I approach an officer and report a missing creek? But then I remember where to find it: slinking under the alley where a restaurant hangs baskets of flowers over the murky, odorous water littered with beer cans.

Strange beauty of a length of muddy fabric curled around a stone. Farther on, behind the bike shop, a crop of white daffodils. At the old ice house, now turned into shops, the creek is studded with islands of dock leaves and flourishing green sedge. I cross a patch of wasteland behind some apartments and find myself on the railroad track once more, watching the creek flow away where I can't follow, underneath the lumberyard where the disused milling company building rises, a shadow of its nineteenth-century splendor, its shattered windows gazing wearily across town.

Why do I love to stand here, where the walls that channel the creek are smeared with graffiti, where my foot almost drops between the railroad ties, where a rotting wooden fence leans crazily, where the water of Blacks Run is so foul and sorry, bubbling brown at the edge? Maybe because the porous surface asserts itself powerfully in this place of rust, abandonment, and decay. A ruined dignity rises from these neglected things, a silent admission that no surface is truly impervious.

"Nothing exists but has a porous texture," wrote the Roman poet Lucretius. Lowering my hood against the thin rain,

I watch Blacks Run slip away toward its destination in the bay—dirty, derelict, impaired, alive.

In the Margin of the Margin

Public space is a border zone, made for everyone and no one. To walk down a sidewalk is to inhabit the margin.

Today the streets sparkle as if fresh from a spa. Over the weekend, a hailstorm pummeled our hills like a cosmic masseuse, followed by a sandpaper wind that scoured the landscape to a brilliant shine. Drenched, frozen, whipped dry, and exfoliated all over, the city gleams. I'm heading up Martin Luther King Jr. Way, walking against the traffic that roars over the hill from the direction of the mall, to take a turn through Old Town.

In the scrubby bank that slopes steeply up from MLK to Ott Street, there's a flight of concrete steps, one of my favorite things in the city. Cars can't cut through here; a bicycle would be something of a liability, as you'd have to carry it up or down; but for a walker, this half-hidden stairway is perfect. It appears suddenly, as if by magic, perpendicular to the sidewalk, inviting: *Come up, come away, get out of the noise!* If the sidewalk is the margin of a neighborhood, a ribbon of public space among private lots, this stairway represents the withdrawn and secret heart of our common territory: the backstage of the street, the margin of the margin.

Climb the steps among the rustling creeper and spindly trees and you will emerge into the quiet of Old Town. In this neighborhood, houses from the late nineteenth to the mid-twentieth century stand in grand, hushed ranks, each one different, all beautifully maintained up here on the hill, windows glittering, graceful gardens trimmed with box and holly.

I don't live here, but I can walk here, among these elegant homes, in the shade of a voluptuous pink magnolia already in bloom, its tulip-shaped flowers balanced like wax candles. I admire the inventive designs of the windows: dormer windows roofed like miniature houses, angled bay windows, French doors, decorative crescent moons. I pass the white house with black trim, the wraparound porch with the huge pillars, the balcony overlooking the Italianate garden, and I feel I know these houses, I've walked here so often. I greet them from the sidewalk and then, when the sidewalk ends in typical Friendly City fashion, from the street, sending a farewell glance toward the attic window where a chair waits, turned toward the view of the mountains, for someone who never comes.

Here's the sign that says Dead End, on which a local wag has stuck the word Grateful. And yes, I'm grateful, because this end is dead only to vehicles. To walkers, it's marvelously alive, because it leads into the alley, a third realm between the private shade of the yards and the public glare of the street.

These alleys form a network of footpaths around the Friendly City. Sometimes they're paved or covered with gravel, as here, in Old Town, where they provide access to garages, and sometimes they're overgrown and nearly impassable, clogged with volunteer saplings, discarded garden equipment, and stacks of wood. The alleys are the margin of the margin, a dreamlike space both held in common and hidden from view. This is one of our greatest treasures. I hate to see an alley blocked, to find myself forced to turn back, tripping over logs and rakes.

A friend once told me a story about a conference at a small Christian university in the Midwest. My friend, who had helped organize the conference, was excited to welcome several guests from Europe for the weekend event. But how horrified these visitors were, my friend told me ruefully, to find that, first of all, the campus was dry, without a single beer garden or cozy pub, and, worse, it was impossible to walk anywhere! "We are good walkers," they insisted. "Just show us the way to town." Brusque, square-shouldered, and shod in excellent leather, these athletic foreign professors gazed with mountaineers' eyes across the fields of grain, but my friend told them reluctantly that they really *could not* walk to town. The problem was not the distance; the problem was that there were no paths.

"No paths? No paths?" the guests repeated in disbelief, color draining from their faces. No, my unhappy friend replied. On the roads, where no one expected to find walkers, the risk of traffic accidents was too high, and if the visitors cut through the farms, they might get arrested or even shot.

This story has stuck with me, the moans of those scholars marooned on a desert campus echoing in my imagination, conjuring visions of an exotic place where pedestrian access is taken for granted: a walker's paradise.

Lovely aqua gate, little gazebo, wicker chairs in the backyards. I walk between fences covered with ivy, passing a swimming pool, the dome of an outdoor pizza oven, stone benches in landscaped arbors, a sweeping stretch of lawn. Even the sheds are adorable here! I wouldn't mind living in one. Pinecones dance in the wind. Forsythia bushes extend their golden froth. The grape hyacinth is blooming. I imagine I planted these flowers, this is my yard, I'm going to read the paper on the screened-in porch. Maybe this is my gabled window, the old glass thick as syrup. I've slipped behind the curtain to dwell in the dark interior. These houses invite dreams that are only possible here, in the margin of the margin, among those who are just passing through, because if I lived in one of these houses, I'd have to keep the windows clean, I'd worry about the age of the bricks, that cracked step would become my problem, and that leaning oak, and the patches of mold on the stucco of the shed, and this overturned canoe scored with rust. I'm grateful to be a passerby, linked to these things by affection rather than ownership, greeting the topiary clipped in the shape of flames, the rose trellis, and the lantern on the wall, only to leave them behind in this space where no one and everyone belongs.

Natural Light

LET'S GO EAST up the hill today, then north along Jackson Street, on this sharp-edged morning, when it feels good to climb up through the alleys flecked with azure speedwell.

Look at this view! I'm at the crest of the hill. If I could walk through the air, I'd step right onto the tops of the spring trees, trees that will soon be so thick with leaves it will look like there can't be a city down below, as if a forest stretches all the way to the mountains.

Walking down Liberty Street, I pass a house with a boarded-up door, then a broad white column that reads Airgas, then an anonymous structure with all its windows closed. Again, as on so many of my walks in the city, the sidewalk disappears. There's no one else here, no palpable human presence, only the vague shapes of faces behind glass in the cabs of the trucks that pass, roaring, pushing hot wind against my hair.

How quickly one comes to the edge of a minor city. The air is transformed by the noise of the trucks, becoming fierce, embattled, smelling of hot rubber and exhaust, making me feel small and out of place. Trucks and detached trailers stand in a parking lot like the silhouettes of a ghost town. I pass a row of buildings I can't identify, windowless things like warehouses with big garage doors, their silent bulk exuding the desolation of some Babylonian ruin.

I shouldn't be here. I should turn around. It feels dangerous walking alone with these trucks juddering past, with nobody else in sight, among these huge objects, the piles of gravel along the railroad track, the stacks of heavy wooden ties, the giant pipes cracked with rust. Under these conditions, the beer cans scattered on the embankment are cheering, human-size things. From what I can see, the neighborhood is partial to a brand called Natural Light. I'm heartened by these signs of life, fortified when I pass a tire shop where a surprised-looking man in overalls gives me a wave, then a child's swing dangling from a sycamore tree near a heap of objects—chairs, hoses, coolers, rakes, a stone gargoyle, a plastic deer. These sparks of human presence give me the courage to go on, past the asphalt expanse of the petroleum cooperative, past the extinguisher store with its nineteenth-century lettering reminiscent of a saloon in an old western, until I reach the Northend Greenway.

Now the bicycle path unrolls before me, smooth as a carpet. It's as if I've passed through a curtain into a great sunlit hall—a spacious, perfumed place filled with the silken rustle of wild teasel. The sky is like a ceiling of blue brocade. Birds trill wildly from the trees. Almost at once a pair of walkers passes me, nodding. "Hi!" I exclaim, amazed at the vitality surging around me: sparrows, finches, honey locusts, people! This is a finished segment of the Northend Greenway, designed, I read on the public works website, as a path for cyclists and walkers, connecting people in the north of the city with "where they want to go." At this point, it can't really connect me with anything—I know from previous experience that it's going to drop me at an inhospitable railroad crossing—but the path itself is worth visiting. The path is a destination, a channel of freshness in the landscape.

Only on the Greenway do I notice how stiffly I've been walking, tensed against the rush of the traffic, breathing small sips of acrid air. Here, my arms swing loose. My lungs expand. I can't shake the feeling that I'm in some grand salon, that these neatly planted trees are pillars, their buds in the sun like lamps. Here's a bench, perfectly placed to listen to the creek burbling in its bed with the sound of a piano playing in the next room. Across the water, the trees bend and sway, heavy with robins like a chorus of hired singers in crimson waistcoats.

The abrupt change between the industrial zone and the atmosphere of the Greenway is not something you can experience from a car. You have to get out in it, to feel the menace of sidling along a road with no sidewalk, then the pleasure and relief of an open path. I think of the yard in my neighborhood, dense with ivy and untrimmed trees, where a sign reads Wildlife Sanctuary. The Greenway, carving out a space where large vehicles can't go, precisely scaled for *Homo sapiens*, is a human sanctuary.

And yet it would be going too far to draw a strict line between the Greenway and the grain elevator rising in the distance. There's nothing more human than a factory. Only we can make a landscape as alienating to the body as a parking lot. If entering the Greenway feels like stepping into a palace, it's because it's crafted, architectural, the product of human effort, developed through city planning, tree-planting volunteers, and donations from local businesses. It's as natural as Natural Light.

Dear Friendly City! I love to see you live up to your name, recognizing that there's more than one way to transform a landscape, restoring your creek, bringing back the birds, creating space for human bodies where we won't be knocked down and crushed by the things we've made, collaborating with plants and animals the way a brewer teams up with hops and fermenting microorganisms, designing corridors of natural light: spaces of sweetness and relaxation, golden as a glass of beer, effervescent with grass-scented air, intoxicating.

Roses, Roots, Branches, Buds

Roses

WHEN YOU FIRST arrived in the city, you were struck by the uncanny atmosphere of the parking lot of Roses Discount Store. That was before you knew the history of this place. Now you can't help wondering: Can a landscape absorb the vibrations of an event? This seems too mystical—surely the destruction of a section of town in the middle of the last century, including a thriving African American neighborhood, cannot actually be imprinted in the bricks of a retail outfit or the plastic shelters of a transit hub. But then why, you wonder, walking past, glancing quickly over your shoulder, why this hollow feeling, this dismay? Is it the size of the parking lot, which always seems too large for the few cars gathered here, creating an eerie, deserted impression? Is it the long, blank wall of the store, filled in with dun-colored concrete where it seems there should be windows? Something in the air here is so blue. You have read stories of people who remember the past of this place, like the resident who said, "It's really funny to go down that part of Mason Street where they tore down beautiful homes and there's nothing, there's a 7-Eleven on the corner." Or Ruth Toliver, who played here as a child: "We rode our bicycles all over town, and everybody knew everybody." She recalled the night of ruin. "We were at the new home on Myrtle Street when my husband, Lowell, came in and said he had just come by Mason Street and saw the original home place being torched. A silence permeated the home as though a family member had died. We could smell the burning no matter where we went in the house."

Roots

YOU WALK UP Gay Street, turn left, then right, and enter Newtown Cemetery. A flag flutters its stars and stripes in the wind. Some gravestones are worn and mossy; others look freshly cut. Nylon flowers adorn them: poinsettias, carnations, roses. Here is a small stone elephant. A cardinal painted pink. A deep hush has settled here, pierced only by birdsong. The houses surrounding the cemetery seem to hold the space in a ceremonial circle, an embrace. At the top of the hill, a sign informs you that African Americans established the community of Newtown after the Civil War, founding this cemetery in 1869, a place open to "all persons of color." Gazing downhill as the sun sends a flimsy radiance through the clouds, you think of your uncle, who came to the Friendly City in the 1970s, leaving his home country of Somalia to study at the Mennonite college a couple of miles from here. You remember a story he told: how he went into town to get a haircut and the white barber told him he couldn't cut your uncle's type of hair, that your uncle would have to go to a certain hill, the barber said, describing the hill with an unrepeatable word, and your uncle, young and alone in the city, found his way to the place, certainly somewhere near here, in the Northeast Neighborhood. Did he walk past this cemetery? What was it like then? It wasn't yet part of the National Register of Historic Places. Did he stop to look at the headstones, did he notice how old they were, did he feel tenderness toward the artificial flowers?

Branches

BEFORE LEAVING the cemetery, you stop at the grave of Lucy F. Simms, the brilliant teacher, born enslaved in 1856, who went on to educate three generations of children. A carved lily extends its leaves from her pale grave marker. The delicate shades of the stone, its gradations from white to dark gray, remind you of a photograph you saw online, a record of Simms's 1905 class, the sober expressions of the children exuding the indefinable, haunting look of old pictures. Their neat collars and upraised heads linger in your mind as you walk farther north, passing the education center named for Simms, so you can almost see their faces superimposed on the kids assembled for some activity on the steps of the building where Simms's work goes on. So history branches over the neighborhood. Here's Ralph Sampson Park, named for the basketball player, another local offshoot. The park is empty today, and you walk alone up the gravel path, through the fine shadows cast by the dangling earrings of a red maple tree, past the picnic shelters, the blue and green futsal court, remembering how you once saw Ralph Sampson downtown at the Italian restaurant. First you thought you saw a man standing at the bar, but then you looked again, caught by something odd in the angle of his limbs, and realized he was sitting, resting an arm on the bar, but he was taller than an ordinary man standing. You remember not wanting to stare, but sneaking a few brief glances, recognizing the most famous person in your town, fascinated by his casual elegance, overwhelmed by the immediate presence of Ralph Sampson: not the history of Ralph Sampson or the errors of Ralph Sampson or even the accomplishments of Ralph Sampson, but the sheer physical fact of Ralph Sampson sitting in a restaurant like other people. *Ralph Sampson!* you thought. *Ralph Sampson!*

Buds

WALKING HOME down Kelley Street, you pause at a quiet, unassuming place: a white house with dark green trim behind a picket fence. There's no sign to mark it, but you know from the address that it's the Dallard-Newman House, once the home of the writer George A. Newman. During his lifetime, Newman wasn't known as a writer. But in the 1870s, he wrote a novel he never published, a 480-page thriller called *A Miserable Revenge: A Story of Life in Virginia*. "A finer estate than that of Joshua Sowers could not be found in all Virginia," the book begins. "We will not give the exact date; let it suffice for us to say we begin our story April the first, in a certain part of the nineteenth century. The morning was a clear, beautiful one. We locate the scene of our story in the county of Frederick, a short distance from the then small town of Winchester. The estate was rightly named Brookland, for the land was covered with brooks." You walk down Gay Street, crossing Blacks Run, in your city that could be described as covered with brooks, tingling with the energy of the old house—for while it's gratifying to live in the hometown of radical educators and basketball stars, the happiest thing for you, of course, is to live in the hometown of a writer.

April

Looping

"You have to be very happy to live in a small city," the Brazilian writer Clarice Lispector once remarked, "because it enlarges happiness just like it enlarges unhappiness."

The wall of a stone house crisscrossed by branches resembles a leopard's pelt in the late afternoon light: an asymmetrical grid of brown and gold. The old house seems muscled like an animal; I would not be surprised to see it flex its shoulder, to watch this streaked fur ripple into life.

I am looping, walking a curved street on the hill above Woodbine Cemetery.

On my left a wide lawn sweeps down to the elegant old bed-and-breakfast garlanded like a wedding cake with balconies and decks, its gravel drive spilling from its doorstep to trace a broad circle like an ancient moat on the green.

Looping, walking a path I've walked before, how many times? In my same jacket, the denim fraying at the cuffs.

The street bends gradually and then more forcefully to the left, striped with alternating bands of lemon yellow and dark gray, the walnuts and cedars casting their shadows over the pavement, their branches weighted with needles or freckled with spring green. The slim, straight trunks rise against the sloping arc of the street, while high in the air the black wires of power lines cut their way across the trees, inking an irregular pattern of rectangles on a blue sky flocked with downy tufts of cloud.

This first impression of the street is abstract, geometrical, the chance meetings of lines and curves oddly suggestive of design, like a chart by a medieval stargazer. The light turns the trunks and utility poles an identical shade of olive, as if the astronomer has sketched them with the same pencil.

As I walk the loop, I enter more fully into the space, my focus narrowing, seeing the man mowing his lawn, the tangled collection of children's bikes, the house with its door wide open so I can peep through to the green at the back, the people trimming trees in their yards or raking out old garden beds, the kids skating in brightly colored helmets.

Bold contrast of the navy-blue house with pale-pink shutters.

A statue of a horse in a backyard, a handsome bay almost the size of a live colt, waiting behind the railing for some romantic escapee to leap from a window, land on its back, and ride into the light.

What's the point of walking a path that goes nowhere, that only brings you back to where you were before?

A row of apartments, peach-brown brick with periwinkle shutters. A woman on a stoop who calls out, "Hey hon, how you doing?" A fantastic garden surrounding an old stone cottage, plants growing right up to the mullioned windows, a superabundance of grasses and vines, the dark red licorice of peony stems, the taut spears of unopened tulips. Baskets, pails, and statues jostle in the greenery as if washed up against the house by a swelling tide—genial frogs with chipped white elbows, the rusty arch of a rose trellis, a bronze child stretching her hand over a pool.

The fact that this street goes nowhere is the reason I like to walk here, to tread the loop, to allow walking to become noticing, passing now the deep ravine that plunges between the backyards, a crack in the land that seems to come from the age of glaciers. Whiteness glints down there where someone has hung clothes on a line. There are plant pots scattered about, piles of bracken and broken barrels, and then the overgrown green hole in the earth, perhaps going down to the creek or even farther, to the planet's core.

Recently, a friend of mine, a resident of the Friendly City for many years, expressed her surprise at how often people move back to this place. They attend one of the universities, go away, then return. They work here for a few years, stray, then retrace their steps. I said, "There must be a magnet in this valley." Maybe it's here, buried in the ragged gorge in the middle of this circular neighborhood, pulling all things toward it, lending an undertone of iron to the tart, nutritious, vegetable scent of the grass.

The valley itself is a loop, a circle. As I complete my own smaller loop, returning to the lawn of the inn, I wonder if it's true, as Clarice Lispector suggested, that small places enlarge what we bring to them. Maybe familiarity creates a kind of magnetism, filling things with significance so they exert a pull on the mind. This rugged old barn on the grass of the inn yard—how often I've stood near it, seeing it covered with snow, masked by twilight so the silhouette of a man on horseback printed on its side fades to smoke, or, as now, lit up by the sun so the torn flag in the window glows with the ghost of its former red.

I walk downhill through the cemetery, feeling I'm being drawn gently into a dim, luminous bowl along with all the flowers—the reddish-purple henbit, the violets scattered like fragments of lapis lazuli, the soft silver clusters of star-of-Bethlehem. When attention moves in a loop, circling around the same small space, it generates force. Walking home down Mason Street, I find this idea reflected in the mural on an apartment building: a chess player with pieces floating above his palm.

Stars surround him. A crescent moon. His board drifts through the galaxy. A game of chess, played on a strict grid, producing a wealth of outcomes—what an image of the power of limited space!

Suddenly I remember looking out the window early this morning: how a single ivory daffodil in the neighbor's yard seemed to make contact, through a long loop of alabaster light, with the Milky Way.

Bookends

THIS WEEK, on a First Friday, when the Friendly City filled with walkers exploring the art and music that sprang up all over downtown, I was struck by the way the character of the city seemed encapsulated in its two bookstores, Parentheses and Downtown Books.

It was the evening of the Chocolate Walk. Many of my fellow pedestrians carried cardboard boxes shaped like oblong houses with peaked roofs, in which they were collecting an array of treats. Shops, galleries, and bars were swept into the storybook atmosphere of a candy factory, united by the warm smell that floated from lighted doorways and the smiles of volunteers handing out bonbons. This year, the Chocolate Walk coincided with a local independent music festival, so that the hordes of sticky-fingered children scrambling toward the next cookie were broken up, like a sea breached by towering rocks, by clumps of tall punks in T-shirts weathered as the sails of shipwrecks, their heads topped with multicolored hairdos like birds of paradise. In the swirling scents of cocoa, mosh pits, and baby shampoo, I realized our downtown was held between two bookstores that exemplified this quirky energy: a mixture of care and chaos, delicate as a sprig of lavender on a truffle and contentedly disheveled as a ripped trench coat.

It's hard to imagine two bookshops more different than the pair that enclose the downtown area like wildly mismatched bookends on a shelf. At one end, close to the pavilion that hosts the farmers market, the decades-old Downtown Books squints from the shadows of the parking garage, its windows plastered with flyers for local music shows, its interior crammed with used books, comics, CDs, and VHS tapes. At the north end, by the poultry plant, Parentheses Books, which opened just last year, displays brand-new volumes in a bright, spacious setting, the rugs on the wood floor echoing the colorful book jackets in muted tones, like reflections in a dim mirror.

At Parentheses, you can sit in a quiet nook and page through your prospective purchases. At Downtown Books, you can barely get down the aisle, which is blocked by crates and stacks of books. Downtown Books belongs to the old city center and possesses the gritty distinction of having survived for nearly fifty years. Parentheses is a new venture, making its home in a pretty shopping arcade that used to be an unprepossessing warehouse (the brainchild of a local magician who also transformed a tire shop into a café and conjured a wine bar out of a random shed nobody had even noticed). At Parentheses, the books are arranged in neat sections, including staff picks and new releases, and the owner and her assistant greet you cheerfully from behind a broad counter that shimmers in the light from the high windows. At Downtown Books, you might completely miss the proprietor, who inhabits a sort of bunker formed from masses of books and CDs; if you want to buy something, clear your throat, and the resident genie will rise from the well, phosphorescent hair and glasses glinting. At Downtown Books, there's almost nothing that costs more than $2.99. A trip to Parentheses could easily leave you thirty bucks poorer (and inestimably happier). At Parentheses, the staff will gladly order a book for you if they don't have it in stock. At Downtown Books, you get what you find.

Despite their differences, these bookends of the city share the most important things: independence, creativity, and character. They bear a human stamp. Walking in, you sense that somebody made this—the way you might feel about artisanal chocolate or a hand-drawn band logo.

Once I visited a coastal city whose downtown was almost devoid of small businesses. Retail spaces had been taken over by the type of chain store usually found in a mall. There was a huge Nieman Marcus. A colossal Banana Republic. How gloomy it was, walking down the main avenue in the golden sunshine, breathing the scent of the nearby sea, and sending brief, appalled glances up at the windows of the soulless titans that had overrun that town.

Shops and restaurants create feelings just like landscapes do. They have their own weather. In the Friendly City, you can bask in the clement glow of Parentheses, browsing surprising new titles, sensing the intelligence behind the selections, the expertise of a curator guiding you like a ranger in the forest. Or you can go spelunking in Downtown Books, among caverns of ancient decorating manuals, garish grottoes of romance novels, and banks built up from yellowed issues of *National Geographic*, where you may unearth some unexpected jewel.

There's an arcadian light at one end of downtown, expressing the city's spirit of cultivation, a desire to make things grow. At the other end, a wind blows through the caves with a bracing chill, exuding a blunt, unsentimental, do-it-yourself energy—a gale on which I can almost hear a gruff voice declare the motto on a postcard I once plucked from a rack of free stuff: Read or Die.

University Walks

THERE ARE TWO WALKS I often take on the campus of the large public university in the Friendly City: the Lake Way and the Hillside Way.

The Lake Way circles Newman Lake in the shadow of the stadium. On this breezy April day, the clouds drift like celestial boats, their white sails reflected in the greenish water. In the warm sun, the air itself feels like water, a luxurious cool stream. The lake appears as calm as a jade carving. Only the Canada geese disturb the surface, turning their dashing black robber masks from side to side and calling out with harsh yelps like a pack of dogs. The Lake Way is brief; in minutes I've reached the road and have to turn back. I extend my excursion by ambling to and fro over the footbridge, greeting some acquaintances out with their dog (we know each other's faces but not names, as is common in the Friendly City), and slipping past a row of dormitories adorned with Greek letters to explore a pedestrian tunnel beside the stream that runs into the lake. Strange signs have been spraypainted in this passageway: an eye, a sun, an abstract human figure. Crouching to keep from knocking my head on the low roof, I feel like an archaeologist who's discovered evidence of a neolithic ritual. When I glance back over my shoulder, I see the lake through the cave mouth, which cuts off the view of the surrounding buildings, creating a scene of somber loneliness, the water lapping at a rocky, deserted shore.

To take the Hillside Way, it's necessary to cross the railroad track, the creek, and the highway, those three great arteries that cut through the Friendly City. At the foot of a hill, near the university bookstore, I pass easily over the first two, hardly thinking about it, the creek trickling discreetly under the sidewalk, the railroad track almost blending into the landscape with its russet tones of dried pine needles. The interstate, though, is another matter. To cross it, I walk on a long bare overpass devoid of shade, exposed to sun and wind, where there's no variation in color to catch the eye, only dull gray asphalt, pale gray concrete, and the tinny gray of the chain-link fence meant to keep me from tumbling down onto the highway. The roar of the traffic below is immense, amplified by the hard surfaces. It's a shock after coming through the west side of campus, where in the fine weather students loll on the quad, ringed by buildings made of the famous local bluestone, shaded by willow oaks, Chinese elms, and the cherry trees decked out in their seasonal pink crepe. On this overpass, seeing, hearing, and feeling are all equally unpleasant. I hunch my shoulders and lower my head against the wind. The whole structure feels wrong, unplanned; surely the first architects of the school did not envision students trudging this noise corridor on their way to and from class.

But grit your teeth and barge across, and walking will become a pleasure again. A hedge of spindle trees, their leaves green and shiny as grapes, welcomes me to the East Campus

Hillside, a project of the university's environmental stewardship initiative. When I take the Hillside Way, following the path down to the creek, I feel time flowing strongly in two directions: toward the future, reflected in the ranks of solar panels that occupy the hilltop, and toward the past, which flickers fitfully in the restored creek bed and the branches of native white oak, black gum, and hickory trees. More than four thousand years ago, I read on the project website, the ancestors of the Monacan Nation camped here by the stream. This place has been a forest, a farm, a pasture, and a lawn, and now it's being coaxed back toward forest again. But time doesn't flow backward, so maybe it's better to think of time here as a spiral, much like the curving paths on the side of the hill, where the little trees, some of them still marked with plastic tags, represent a projection rather than a return of the old woodland. They are thin yet, barely screening the pagoda-like recreation center from view, and providing almost no protection from the din of the highway traffic. Shaking in the wind, as if still breathless from being transplanted, these child trees look about them in wonder, the red maple bashful in its pink dress edged with green, the serviceberry's white ribbons trembling all over.

If, like me, you are not particularly knowledgeable about trees, I recommend taking your university walk with a copy of the online tree guide. With this tool, you can give yourself a rough course in tree identification. You can begin to greet these serene, rustling strangers by name—the purple-leaved plum in severe brown silk, the cucumber magnolia extending its branching array of enameled champagne flutes. Walking uphill toward the campus buildings, passing the twin ponds, peering down to see the family of turtles sunning themselves on a pipe, I breathe the spicy scent of the pines. I linger under a willow tree that tosses its heavy tresses as if bleaching them in the light. I think of the writer Marcel Proust, who wrote, "Soaring and erect, amid the vast offering of their branches, and yet rested and calm, the trees, through their strange and natural posture, invite us with grateful murmurs to feel kinship with a life so ancient and so young, so different from ours and yet appearing as its dark and inexhaustible reservoir."

An outdoor amphitheater has been built into the side of the hill, its small stage encircled by white stone benches. I imagine performances are held here sometimes, but today it's empty, providing a perfect spot for a passerby to stop and declaim, like an impromptu poem, the beautiful names of the trees down below: sweetgum, hornbeam, river birch, sycamore, yellowwood, black tupelo, loblolly pine.

Redbud

Look at this row of redbuds! Stunning—the clusters of violet-pink flowers blooming right on the branches, bursting from the bark. The word *redbud* fully describes the blossoming tree, a single color devoid of green: the special austerity, the purity of the redbud.

Weeks ago, it appeared they had bloomed, when dabs of brightness came out along the branches. But now the flowers are so incredibly thick, the branches no longer look speckled with color—they're layered, smothered, the flowers not buttoned on like dogwood blooms but piped on as if by an expert pastry chef, so that the branches, the trunks, and certain entire streets of the Friendly City are frosted with fabulous pink icing.

The redbud is a native tree; it grows here like a weed. How can something so gorgeous come so cheap? Grizzled redbuds stand before the old high school, their flowers vivid against the tawny brick, the green cannon of the veterans' memorial, the flashing tints of the traffic on High Street. On this warm afternoon, their creamy magenta seems like a visible manifestation of the heat, pulsing in the light-blue, faintly humid, silky sky, where clouds stray, some in puffs like stuffing pulled out of a cushion, others vapory like streaks left behind on a freshly cleaned window.

I have heard that the redbud is sometimes called the Judas tree, and that people often plant it next to a dogwood, which is associated with Christ. The dogwood flower has the shape of a cross, and a small crown of thorns can be discerned in its center; a legend says the cross was made from the wood of this tree. As for the Judas tree, folklore holds that Judas Iscariot hanged himself from a redbud, whose flowers were stained with shame or blood. I take this to mean there's nothing sacred about a redbud. It's the tree of flawed, fallen humanity. In this valley, it grows everywhere.

The redbud sprouts in narrow yards, among the little houses across High Street, up against the porches crowded with grills, bicycles, and brooms, in the knot of lanes that dead-ends against the railroad track—a neighborhood with a youthful feel, maybe because it's near the university, or because the dingy siding and abandoned soccer balls evoke young families with lots of energy and little ready cash. Or maybe it's simply because young people have to live somewhere, and it's hard to imagine a young person buying a house on the other side of High Street, where the yards are larger and the residences statelier, in this town where housing prices have doubled in less than a decade. So I imagine they're here, the young folk, that these are their hammocks and ping-pong paddles under the redbuds. And when I cross High Street and enter the Sunset Heights neighborhood, I picture an older population, people who have lived here long enough to cultivate the gardens smelling pungently of mulch.

Tall, rangy redbuds let down their purple hair in these landscaped bowers, among the stone birdbaths and beds of pansies, as they do among the dandelions and forgotten, mold-spotted sneakers on the other side of High Street. The redbud listens at kitchen windows all over the Friendly City. It sees our shadows pass through the rooms in the grayish early morning. It is there when the red stove light comes on, when the coffee maker clears its throat, when the open refrigerator door throws a band of cold whiteness over the tiles. It hears our groans, our cheers, our laughter, our complaints. Someone says, *I can't run up any more debt.* A child squeals, *It's my birthday!* Someone steps out onto a porch, eyes glazed, too startled by love to notice the brilliant blooms. Someone clutches a banister shaded by a redbud branch outside the window, wondering: *How, after all my work, has it come to this?* In the bruised light of the flowering tree, someone sits down carefully on a porch step, stunned by a sudden pain.

From a luscious cake—its edible blossoms adding a sweet tang to our salads—the redbud will morph into a barbed insect, its branches tipped with greenish, red-veined spikes. Next, the heart-shaped leaves will come, filling out the tree, which will turn into a rustling, many-tiered palace, the fringes of its seedpods hanging down like carpets flung over the balconies. Finally, when the leaves fall, only the seedpods will remain, rattling dryly in the wind like fairy slippers hung up after a dance. What will have happened during all those months? Where will we be then?

The redbud in our yard was a castoff, a switch about two

feet long pulled from a tree a few miles away at our uncle's house. We stuck it in the ground, and almost overnight, it seemed, it became a luxuriant, leafy tree. I continue to be surprised at the height of this tree, its rapid growth. I delight in its spring color filling the little front yard, its frilled parasol that shades the porch on hot afternoons, and its benevolent influence that reaches even the interior of the house, when, at seven o'clock on a summer evening, the lavish, flamelike shadows of the leaves play over the curtains, the floor, the coffee table, the piano, and the wall opposite the sinking sun, imparting a coolness and liveliness to the whole house, an alternation of sun and silhouette so appealing, and so essentially a part of the long twilights, that I remember the time before the redbud tree with a scandalized feeling. How did we ever put up with the dry glare of a treeless sunset in midsummer? How sad the yard was then—a bald square like a postage stamp stuck to the street! I love the redbud for its range, its brazen occupation of space, and its cunning will to transform its surroundings, which we battle by pulling up the volunteer seedlings it drops all over the place and hacking back the branches that threaten to engulf the sidewalk.

May

Things Have More to Tell

LET'S STRAY. Let's wander through the Friendly City on this sunny afternoon in the dogwood season, all the way across town, south to Purcell Park, even if there are other parks closer to home and we have no known acquaintances in this neighborhood. Absorb this place, this day: hot light, cool breeze, the dark-blue scalloped edge of the mountains rising against the sky over Port Republic Road, the beautiful smell of the trees all along the quiet streets near the park where other people live, where the aura of unknown lives colors the air.

A brick wall guarded by plaster eagles and lions. A blue-gray residence set far back on a velvet lawn, winking its arched windows. At the top of the rise, a baronial place with huge white columns surveys the neighborhood with noble condescension. Only one house on this street shows any activity today, but, as if to make up for the sleepy air of the other gardens, this one spot bustles with life. A determined-looking young man wheels a barrow back and forth across a yard covered with straw; at the foot of the driveway, a dozen shrieking children swarm over a mound of mulch.

To the neighborhood kids, it must seem as if a minor alp has materialized overnight. Fully dressed or in pajamas, barefoot or shod, uniformly dusty, they trample over the mulch hill, try to slide down it, climb it again and again. The discovery of the mysterious mountain electrifies the street. I think of Walter Benjamin, who wrote about children's love for things abandoned by adults, especially "the detritus generated by building, gardening, housework, tailoring, or carpentry." It's not that children want to imitate grown-ups, Benjamin thought; rather, in the stuff strewn around adult workplaces, children "recognize the face that the world of things turns directly and solely to them." Elsewhere he wrote: "Finds are to children what victories are to adults."

I read his words in a book by the philosopher Laura U. Marks, who extends his line of thought: "Simply," she writes, "things have more to tell people than most people have time to hear..."

I walk down to the park, thinking of children and play, and of the wonderful gesture of Edward S. Purcell, who in 1954 sold his land to the city for one dollar on the condition that it would be used as a playground and public recreation area. The symbolic fee paid for the land that would become Purcell Park makes the exchange feel like a game, a mischievous transaction with play money. Passing the tennis courts, I glimpse the ash-brown turrets of the Kids Castle, where a few children are clambering about.

A gap in a thicket catches my eye. Beyond it, in the whispering shade, a restored stretch of the creek swells and burbles. This is Blacks Run like I've never seen it before, broad and full, barred with the shadows of branches, green with reflected foliage. Across town, where I live, I've never imagined the creek could hold so much water. As I walk beside it on a trail carpeted with glossy celandine, a duck starts from the shadows and flies a few yards downstream—no, not a duck, something larger, more elegant, a flicker of stormy blue. I creep along the water's edge, following the bird as it watches me and rises to glide farther down the creek, keeping its distance. Is it a heron? A cormorant? It draws me through a swath of wildflowers that runs like a mosaic beside the creek: purple clusters of dame's rocket and coral bells of buckeye on an emerald ground. When I lose sight of it, I stand among mustard blooms.

Laura U. Marks draws a distinction between the material world and the simulated worlds of digital media. Interactive media like search engines and videogames evoke a feeling of infinite possibility, she writes, but what users encounter in them is "only quantitatively new." To encounter something truly fresh, *qualitatively* new, you're better off looking out the window than at your laptop screen, "because when you look out the window, your perception may bring something into being that never existed that way before."

Look out your window. Wander into a place you've never been. I think of the children crawling sedately through the Kids Castle, and those other children up the street, stamping their naked feet in the mulch, crowing and dancing in transports of delight. The Kids Castle is fun, but it doesn't provoke that heady joy, the shock of seeing the face that the world of things turns directly and solely to children. To see that face, the children must worm their way into places where they're not supposed to be: garden sheds, kitchens, the muddy brink of a creek.

And what of the grown-up people? The world of things may no longer turn its face to us, but by walking aimlessly—which might be our form of play—perhaps we can catch the glimmer of its eye. This spray of golden drops, which some have compared to the kingdom of heaven—what does it have to tell?

Transient Feeling

SEASON OF LUSHNESS. Everything green, burgeoning. You go down certain streets you know, the ones with the big old houses where the students live. Tangles of fairy lights and streamers hang from the pillared porches, drooping in knots like overburdened branches.

This transient feeling, a sense of exuberant life. Students on the porches, it's eighty degrees and cloudy, it'll rain later, now there's a thin sun, they're laughing, swinging lazily in hammocks, tossing empty bottles down into the grass, and what's this joy?

These houses are so spacious, so handsome, they almost look imposing—but then suddenly there's a bent awning streaked with rust, a crude spraypainted stone in the yard, a flight of crumbling steps with the tiles falling off. Once you've identified the place as a student house, it loses its grandeur. It comes down to earth. The walls are bashed about the edges, roughly used like old soccer cleats. You notice the bare, scrubby yards, the flaking trim exposing layers of paint, the bushes chopped back with a careless hand. A red plastic cup in the weeds reminds you of how you once saw a groundskeeper casually mowing over such cups in one of these yards, his fixed gaze expressing infinite boredom, his machine spitting out splinters of red and white plastic along with the grass.

Neglected buildings, unloved and shabby, serving temporary tenants. Yet there's something wonderful about the student houses: a distinctive energy, perhaps more intense for being seasonal, that adds its special zest to the city. The students give names to their houses and paint them on signs: Uptown, Narnia, The Funk House, The Tree Haus, The Planetarium. They fill the porches with sagging couches, lock their bikes and scooters to the railings, decorate the doors with goofy dolls or plastic skulls. Here's a venerable old dump with a sign announcing "Established in 1905." Dandelions spangle the yard like coins. Here's a tire swing on a rope, a folding chair face-down on the grass, a sunroom crammed with exercise equipment.

The Friendly City is home to two universities. Students make a difference in this modest town, swelling and shrinking the population in ways that can't be missed, as the Bradford pear trees thicken with starry, funky, unruly blossoms. Every autumn the city releases a collective, fairly good-natured groan: *The students are back!* Traffic doubles; café tables fill; lines for weekend brunch snake down the street. And now, in spring, as the students begin to decamp, you can feel the migration, an increased bustle and tension in the air. Bags of trash pile up on the curb. Flattened cardboard boxes lean against steps or splay in the driveways, softened by rain.

What's this joy? It's not relief that the students are going away—on the contrary, you're charmed by their presence, their vitality, amused even by their invasion of parking spots, their distracted driving, their reckless habits on skateboards and scooters, their noise. What can explain the buoyancy you feel on your walk, passing houses already deserted by their inhabitants, the curtainless windows exuding a lonely air, the grayish wood of the porches bare but for a stray plastic crate or a stack of two-by-fours? The can of hairspray, the broken sink, the blinds slung at an angle—why does happiness flow from such sad things? It must be a feeling of possibility, you think, rounding the corner: a sense of openness, of potential.

Transience of the spring flowers, transience of the students, transience and luster of the season. They are going away, moving on, perhaps temporarily, to study abroad or spend the summer at home, perhaps for good, making their way uncertainly to other places, to unfamiliar demands and a new sense of time. Those who have left school will begin to live by a different clock: not the cyclical ebb and flow of the semester system, but the steady stream of workdays laid like tracks to the horizon or the rushed and panicky rhythm of underemployment. Most will not have again the feeling of *happy* transitoriness, something they've taken for granted up to now, the sense that things are ending and it's right that they should end, as summed up in the common expression "It's just a phase." At some point, one ceases to be offered the grace of living in phases, you realize as you pass a yard where an overflowing trash can totters on a mound of refuse: something the city's residents are (just) willing to tolerate from students but would never stand for in a long-term neighbor.

It's right, of course, that custom puts an end to the period when such behavior can be excused as a passing stage. And yet one does not cease to change. Maybe that's the secret of the sparkling feeling that fills you as you walk past these forsaken, junk-strewn porches. If the hills of the Friendly City offer an altered experience of space, the student houses do the same for time. Climb a rise to look out on the folds of the mountains; contemplate the torn screen of a house marked "Off-Campus Housing for Rent" to renew your sense of the future.

A Dead Sweet Perfume

"Why must we always use only our sight, and never our smell or taste to study a city?" the poet Federico García Lorca wondered.

If you live in the Friendly City, you are familiar with *the smell*—a thick, rank odor that sometimes descends on our streets, especially after rain.

Ever since moving here, I've longed to acquire the bumper sticker I see from time to time that reads "I ♥ Dog Food Smell." I'm told they're no longer available. I imagine a short-lived project, perhaps sponsored by the city, that produced this whimsical badge of civic pride. These bumper stickers must have been popular for a time—I certainly would have bought one—but eventually, I suppose, they came to be regarded as silly or even embarrassing, and were discontinued, as we so often leave behind childhood friendships that have failed to fit into our adult lives: the ones with weird people, the ones that were too intense, the ones in which we were most fully ourselves.

Each inhabitant of the city must discover the smell. Every child born here must sense it for the first time. Students settling into university life wake up one day with a startled look, testing the air in brief, cautious sniffs. What—what—is that *smell*? An entertaining article from several years ago claims to have solved the mystery of the odor that fills our streets on cloudy, lukewarm afternoons, causing dismay in those who expected to breathe the fresh air of the mountains. No, it's not a puppy farm. It's not dead chickens, livestock, or—as one particularly inventive rumor has it—a factory where dogfood is manufactured from horsemeat. It's the chickenfeed supplied to the city's poultry plants, described in the article as "a mix of molasses, corn, and other organic materials."

Molasses? Corn? The city should smell like grits and syrup. Instead—maybe as a result of those vaguely sinister "other organic materials"—its air seems to remind everyone of dogs. Muddy dogs, damp dog hair, dogfood stored in a humid pantry. Walking past the poultry plant near my house on a dull, stormy afternoon, I'm plunged in this muggy, canine reek, hugged by it, bowled over as if by exuberant pets, assailed by hot panting breath.

What does it smell like, precisely? Can you describe its layers? It wafts out over the place where gravestones are sold, it buoys the turkey vultures circling over the plant, their wings outspread on a fug redolent of feet, of sweaty gym socks. It rolls like a wave on the breast of the creek, where I pause for a moment to watch the rain-swollen current swirl over a discarded No Trespassing sign—something that seems like a good joke today, a defiance of border control very much in harmony with this cheddary musk that acknowledges no frontiers. It is seeping into the auto repair shop, infusing the biscuits and gravy at the popular local restaurant across the street, fingering the knickknacks in a window, slipping between the hydraulic hoses at the equipment rental store.

A dusty scent with a saccharine edge and a sour, curdled center. As I walk, I'm becoming a sommelier of the smell. My palate picks up notes of cheese and crackers left in the heat on the dashboard of a car. I sense overtones of a big dark-amber barn full of chaff that makes you cough. A bulky, viscous body, weighed down by rain-dense air. Yes, my city smells like a barn in the rain, but with a nearly unbearable, gamey finish, a stink that makes you want to draw your head back sharply, as if you've shoved your face deep in an animal's pelt.

I think of the flutter of nerves in my department at the university the last time we hired a new professor. How anxious we were, planning a welcome party for this colleague who had just arrived in town. Would it rain? Would it smell? Should we risk dinner on my back patio, so near the complex that gives off this fearful stench? Our conversation was protective, I now realize, not of our new colleague, nor of our personal pride, but of the city. We feared exposing the less flattering aspects of our town before the stranger had had a chance to fall in love.

Can you capture the smell in words? Recently, reading the autobiography of W. E. B. Du Bois, I was struck by his description of rural Georgia: "Back toward town we glided, past the straight and thread-like pines, past a dark tree-dotted pond where the air was heavy with a dead sweet perfume."

Maybe that's it: a dead sweet perfume. I cross a slender tributary of the creek that runs between green backyards, spanned by a little wooden bridge, and think how nice it would be to have this rill run past your porch, like living on the banks of a tiny private river. A picnic table drowses in the shade. Full-fleshed carmine roses flank a gate, their color throbbing against the grass. Everything is permeated by the sweet-sour, oppressive, old-meat smell—a smell that surely, if I were ever unlucky enough to move away from the city, would become a wellspring of nostalgia.

In Deep Time

ON THIS CLOUD-FLECKED DAY, the city wears its summer palette: green and gray with occasional pops of brighter color. Walking uphill from Chicago Street, I pass heaps of gravel from building projects, mouse-colored walls, trees in full leaf, light-green lawns. In the general tints of gray and green, flashes of stronger pigment stand out: a yellow bulldozer motionless in its Sunday sleep, orange cones around the construction sites, a lava-pink plastic bag, a porch aflame with geraniums.

Wind in the trees. I'm walking up toward the water tower at the Mennonite university, through a sleepy, squeaky-clean neighborhood, the houses ringed by well-kept gardens of pansies, marigolds, and catmint. There's a yard full of tumbling moss, another dusted with pinkish-gray clover. It's one of those days when you can really breathe. The breeze sweeps away the odor of the poultry plants, a fresh stream of air that seems to come directly from the mountains, bud-scented and balmy, flowing through a mellow atmosphere just touched with golden light.

In the Friendly City, there are days that are too hot and days that are too cold, but also an extraordinary number of perfect days: hours of light so inviting, tranquil, and refreshing, it's almost startling how well they fit the human form. As I walk up behind the brick buildings of the small university, entering the delicious coolness of the trees, an awareness of deep time tingles on my skin. We have grown together for thousands of years: the hills, the trees, the air, and me. In the variegated swirl of light and shade beneath the leaves, I feel it in my marrow: I was made for this planet.

I think of this as a fairy-tale feeling, after the scholar Max Lüthi, who points out that the protagonists of fairy tales—often small, poor, and weak—find aid and comfort in the natural world. Birds fly down from the trees to warn them of danger. Fish spring from the fountains to offer advice. A river lowers its waters to let the wanderer cross. Fairy tales, writes Lüthi, represent the human being as vulnerable and isolated, but with "the capacity for universal relationships." A child in these stories can make friends with anything in the world: a dramatization of the fundamental link between human and nonhuman life.

I tramp uphill on a path of pebbles, its cream and ochre stones reminding me of the bread little Hansel drops in the forest, making me think of the German-speaking settlers in this valley, like the Mennonites who founded this university. When they came to this place, did they feel a resonance in the landscape? I remember once, on a trip to Nevada, learning about the large Basque community there, who were drawn to that rugged, elevated region because it resembled their native Pyrenees. I wonder if the German speakers who came here felt a similar pull, a sense of rapport with these green hills and cloud-hung skies. As I reach the peak, the keen, exhilarating breeze rushes into my face, and I look out on hills in both directions: toward town, above a sea of leaves interspersed with factory towers, the steel-blue crest of Massanutten; on the other side, dark banks of trees rolling into the distance, dissolving into a hazy, silver-topped ridge.

I have read that many early settlers in this valley were Germans from the Palatinate, an area of southern Germany that, according to an online image search, looks remarkably like the view from the top of this hill. I imagine they felt their stories would suit this place: ancient tales of buried treasure, of diminutive men digging in the hills, of the lost child searching for the glass mountain who sees the kindly stars around her, each one sitting on its own little chair.

Stories like these are the oldest tales we know, reaching back as far as human history, laced with myth, philosophy, and the earliest science. According to some scholars, the seven dwarfs in the tale of Snow White are related to the seven planets of medieval astronomy and the seven noble metals of the alchemists. They are spirits of the hills, their daily round taking them into the depths of the earth in a reflection of the celestial circle. We can read, in these friendly little men, a vision of the whole cosmos coming to the aid of a single lonely child.

Fairy tales express the feeling of having evolved with and for a landscape. They are stories of deep time. If German settlers found a place for their stories in these hills, and if the Scots-Irish who came around the same time also felt an interior chord at the sight of green cliffs under a misty sky, how strong the bond must be that links the Monacan Nation to this valley after millennia of coevolution. Walking back downhill, I think of the story told by a young Monacan dancer, a tale that took shape in the dance she performed in a dress decorated with 365 jingling metal cones. A dance of days, of time, of the turning of the year. A man's daughter was ill, the dancer said, and no one could heal her. One night the unhappy father had a dream in which he saw a dress covered with shimmering cones. "The cones jingled against one another, making beautiful music as the dress swayed upon an ethereal form." The man asked his wife to make such a dress and dance beside their sick child. And when the daughter heard the jingling, she was cured.

The Language of the Flowers

"What is natural about being human?" asks the poet Harryette Mullen. "What to make of a city dweller taking a 'nature walk' in a public park while listening to a podcast with ear-bud headphones? What of a poet who does not know the proper names of native and non-native fauna and flora, who sees 'a yellow flower by the creek'—not a *Mimulus*?"

Mullen's words imply a certain self-criticism, an embarrassment at being an urban poet who doesn't know the scientific terms for plants and animals, whose cyborg body is hooked up to plastic and silicon, whose "nature walk" hardly deserves the name. I'm thinking of this as I cross the street from the state university and enter the trail through the woods that leads to the arboretum, carrying some of the poet's wistfulness along with me, her very modern melancholy.

I am a city walker like Mullen, equipped with a phone that takes photographs, an app that identifies plants, and another that recognizes bird sounds. Without these technological supports, I wouldn't be able to tell you that the brief, fluent whistle I hear in the depths of the leaves is a red-eyed vireo, or call the pimple-pink, coarsely furred wineberry by its name. Breathing the moist, shady air, waving off the gnats, I walk through a space that's like me: a hybrid of the biological and the artificial, the wild and the engineered. A wide gravel path welcomes the tread of my sneakers; between the hoary old trunks that plunge high into the sky, upholding a humid canopy, I glimpse wan strips of parking lot and the backyards of people who live near the trail: brick patios, sunlit deck chairs, potted ferns.

What is natural about being human? An orange post in the undergrowth blazes "Warning: Buried Fiber Optic Cable." A gnomelike trashcan stands discreetly in the fallen leaves, wrapped in a grandmotherly shawl of black plastic. Farther on, a field of colored flags marks an ongoing project, labeled by a nearby sign as a Native Shade Garden. This hybrid environment comes to a head in the arboretum, where a wooden bridge arcs among trees tagged with nameplates, where the screeches of jays are interspersed with the shrieks of children playing around the giant mushroom statues in the green sunglow.

The humans are here, the young, the elderly, humans with walkers, humans with canes, in strollers, in backpacks, toddling unsteadily on little plump legs, bending to read the signs on the trees, crying out at the sight of a turtle, crouching to watch fish dart below the filmy surface of the pond. They gather in eager groups around the flowers. "Oh, look at this one!" they exclaim. "Look at that!" And what do the flowers say? How many people here have brushed up on their botanical Latin, how many are themselves gardeners with an intimate knowledge of growing things, how many are simply drawn to pink and blue, to a melting whiteness, to a soft fragrance, as naturally as a swarm of bees?

I've brought along a little book that was given to me as a child: a glossary of the Victorian language of the flowers. Once, as I understand it, a certain refined, repressed, almost pathologically subtle subculture communicated through bouquets. Hearts were broken and engagements negotiated through combinations of color and scent, sometimes accompanied by restrained gestures, such as holding a nosegay upside down or at the level of one's heart. Paging through the book as I walk, I learn that the dogwood blooms, with their stiff, regular petals of white leather, are saying *Durability*. They are speaking, I think, of an endless love, because I can't imagine a time when humans no longer prize, cultivate, and gravitate toward flowers.

The peony says *Bashfulness*, nodding its oversized head, heavy with mortification and stained with blushes all over its hot cheeks. The haughty spiderwort announces *Esteem not love*, keeping suitors at a distance with long, fastidious green fingers, drawing back its pinched purple face above an elaborate choker of jade beads. *Rendezvous*, says the chickweed, winking its impudent hazel eyes surrounded by starry white lashes. I laugh at this complex code from the past, finding it ridiculous that the rhododendron, its papery mauve flowers looking faint with heat, is supposed to be shouting *Danger! Beware!* And the mountain laurel—so familiar to me from hikes in the national forest it seems domestic and cheerful in its red-and-white gingham topped with a snowy apron—this companionable flower, I'm told, signifies *Ambition*.

But all our codes are arbitrary. Flowers have no proper names. For this magnificent iris, its mink collar splashed with overpoweringly sweet cologne, the word proposed by my little book—*Flame*—will do just as well as *Iris germanica cultivars*. Flowers are multilingual, speaking horticultural Latin to those who can understand it, addressing themselves to others with form and color. They say *yellow*. They murmur scent. They communicate through silken texture, irritating pollen, milky fluids, and thorns.

On the hillside, a field of bachelor's buttons dazzles me with its blue, the flowers upright on their stalks like gallants at a ball, proclaiming *Celibacy* as if to remind me, with a merry glance, that they have their own way of life, which is not mine—while scattered among them, a few bold poppies raise their scarlet bowls, each smoldering vessel sprinkled with charred spices, bearing a message that applies equally to human language games and the brilliant world of flowers: *Fantastic extravagance*.

June

Work in Progress

Dear friend,

You ask me to tell you what I love most about my town. How to describe this place to you, who have never been here? Is it possible to convey the feeling of walking in my city so that even a trace of it will reach you?

There is a house in my neighborhood we call Finnegans Wake, after James Joyce's famously challenging novel. During his many years writing this book, Joyce called his manuscript *Work in Progress*—a name that suits my neighbor's unpredictable, chaotic residence, where a number of projects are going on at any given time: a car raised on jacks, a massive tree being gradually reduced to logs, rows of planters half filled with dirt.

I wonder if it will surprise you to hear that if you visited me and asked to go on one of my favorite walks, I wouldn't take you to any of the parks. We wouldn't survey the picturesque grounds of the two universities or head downtown to the Saturday farmers market. Instead, I'd take you around my neighborhood, down Willow Street, into the angle formed by two main roads: Market Street, generally known as 33, and the heteronymous thoroughfare that has so many titles (High Street, Virginia Avenue, Harpine Highway) there is no point in calling it anything but 42.

In this sheltered nook between busy roads, we'd find the air I love to breathe, the inimitable essence of the city. These streets have a stillness, a somnolence, almost an aura of suspended animation, that encourages a relaxed yet heightened awareness, as in dreams. Above all, their unfinished quality enchants me—and I believe it expresses the spirit of this place in a profound way. The city lives in these old unpainted wooden steps, the dried wreath on the wall, the yawning screen door, the faded banner that reads Home Sweet Home.

How often I've walked these streets on days like today, fine and dry, the light clear gold, almost silver, pale and plentiful as bindweed, my steps uneven, urged on by the rousing breeze but slowed by my longing to look at every single house along my route. I immerse myself in these unhurried, ragtag works in progress. The rusty shutter, crooked on a white wall. Scattered cinderblocks, a gap-toothed fence, a plant pot lying on its side, bags of topsoil under a porch swing. The planks, everywhere, stacked on the porches, leaning against walls, the anonymous chunks and slats that will surely be useful for something, the mops and buckets, the lengths of pipe, extension cord, and wire, the pile of gravel beside a mysterious hole in a driveway. I pass a neighbor working on a brick wall with casual, almost leisurely movements. An empty garden bed, parched earth with a few thin weeds. A bathtub on a porch. From a distant street comes the low, murmurous, unending sound of summer: the drone of a mower.

I wonder, dear friend, if you would enjoy standing here with me in the shade of a mulberry tree whose fruit has blackened the sidewalk, facing this tiny house sunken in its gloomy, sloping yard, where a cat gazes warily from a curtainless window. I'm trying to understand my own attachment to cracked concrete, fractured storm windows, and disorderly piles of stuff. After all, there are plenty of well-groomed houses on this street, their gardens crisp paintboxes of lilies and petunias—why am I drawn to signs of incomplete or inexpert work, shoddy compromises, and abandoned projects? A plastic-covered dormer window smothered in the boughs of a hickory tree, ancient bicycle frames hanging in the damp darkness of a porch, heaps of furniture crowded into garages, tables on top of chairs, a chipped ceramic owl perched on a lampstand—these are the sights that can stop me in my tracks. The angel statue toppled in the chicory sparks my imagination more than many grander works of art. And while I can admire a trim, shipshape house and yard, such places often feel a bit cold and dull—until, that is, I catch sight of a tumbledown shed in the backyard or a broken blind winking from an upstairs window.

There is a scruffiness to the Friendly City that might come from a lack of money or time or both, from a lack of ambition or initiative—but it might also stem from a certain ease, a contentment with incremental change, an acceptance of mess because there are young children in the home, a tolerance for transitional states since you can't afford a professional so you just tinker with things on your own, understanding that a work in progress takes the time it takes. Maybe the city has made an unconscious, collective decision to embrace shabbiness. Maybe that says something bad about us, or maybe it says something good, but at any rate it's a recognizable feeling in our neighborhoods, a muted but consistent energy.

What is the beauty of the unfinished? How is a feeling of restfulness and resilience produced by raw boards, blistered paint, and bales of chicken wire? Here are a few possibilities:

- The beauty of animation. A deflated kiddie pool hanging over a railing, a crumpled sweatshirt, sneakers jumbled together, a skateboard, a shovel, an office chair: Someone here is alive.
- The beauty of invention. The fallen porch swing, trailing its chains, remains parked on the stoop with its cushions, transformed into a bench.
- The beauty of making do. At the end of the street, two overhead wires hold a blunt wedge of wood, left behind when the tree was cut down. Apparently, this piece of wood couldn't be removed safely. It hangs there, not ideal but good enough.
- The beauty of acceptance. If you came over to my house, would you want to find me wearing lipstick and neurotically sweeping the place? Wouldn't you rather get a welcome hug from a friend in a baggy T-shirt and settle into a couch softened by a rumpled old throw? This collection on a porch—a battered cabinet, window boxes, a stool, a birdcage, a cooler with paper plates on top—it says, I accept myself, cluttered and under construction as I am. I accept you, too. Yes, even your shed.

Love ever...

The Musical City

Song of the Open Window

The June heat brings changes to the soundscape of the city. Winter is muffled and still; summer is loud, brash, and tuneful. Snatches of music blare from car windows, the Doppler effect making ripples of sound in the streets. Walking downtown, we pass a group of vehicles stopped at a red light, drawn together in a discordant, competitive chorus. Hip-hop beats with Spanish lyrics interweave with melancholy country guitars, the intricate African twang of banjos, the rockslide of heavy metal. When the light changes and the cars move on, they will make their way through neighborhoods where even the flowers seem to announce the arrival of music season: magenta and rust-colored echinacea to keep away summer colds, fragrant elderflower for a throat-soothing cordial, and all the big, showy blooms—sensitive hydrangeas in pink or blue lace, princely ornamental yuccas, the glamorous ivory satin magnolia—that are the divas of the vegetable kingdom.

Ah! How Sweet

We have come downtown for a free concert at the Methodist church whose imposing gothic tower soars above the nearby buildings. Within this somber edifice of dark-brown stone, a cheerful crowd has gathered for the noon concert, one of a series that will run all week as part of the annual Shenandoah Valley Bach Festival. The festival offers a good deal more than Bach—during this hour, we hear dynamic works by lesser-known composers, a contemporary violin concerto with an ecological theme, a lyrical modern piece that transports us to an imagined seacoast, and a moving interpretation of the spiritual "Motherless Child." All at no cost, available at the end of a short walk. One violinist, introducing a series of brief movements, compares it to a box of truffles, offering pleasures to suit every palate: candied canzonetta, piquant scherzo, gooey berceuse. I think of Bach's comical *Coffee Cantata*, in which a young caffeine addict enthuses, "Ah! how sweet coffee tastes!" How sweet this music tastes, how delicious it is to be treated to this feast of sound in a church like a candy box with an elegant white lid, where the performers, their instruments polished to a caramel sheen, are surrounded by wood-paneled walls like well-tempered chocolate, poised on a matte red carpet like strawberry fruit leather, and bathed in the reflected light of a magisterial pipe organ that glitters like silver paper.

Sing It Yourself

WALKING HOME, we pass the Court Square Theater, the Friendly City's independent cinema and performance space. Eraser-pink crests decorate the wall, wheels and grinning animals bearing ornate shields that read RMC, recalling the building's former life as the Rockingham Motor Company. These emblems work well for a theater, the canine heads like masks, the wheels suggesting the temporal aspect of performance, the curtain's rise and fall. We remember shows we've seen here, projects created by and for the community. There was the play about the traumatic expulsion of families from the mountains in the 1930s, its emotion heightened by the fact that several actors were descended from those families, and by the folk music that filled the stage: square dances, fiddle tunes, gospel melodies. There was a comedy written by a local duo that attracted the city's punks in droves, so that the theater seemed ready to burst with laughter and black mascara—for the Friendly City is home to a vibrant underground music scene that thrives in basements through the efforts of passionate volunteers. In fact, our city boasts a show house so old—more than thirty years, an astounding length of time in this chancy, irregular subculture—it's been compared to the Roman Colosseum. (We have heard that this storied venue is about to be shut down, but we can neither confirm nor deny the rumor. To catch what may be the final show at this legendary house, and to learn where its inevitable successor will emerge, you will have to—as the flyers put it—ask a punk.)

Distant Echoes

IF WE COULD, we'd walk to the springs of music scattered throughout the surrounding woods and fields, whose echoes reach us here in the city. We've heard reports of a "hootenanny" that regularly takes place in a neighboring forest. Churches ring with Sunday harmonies throughout the valley. As we walk down Main Street, nearing home, a shop sign invites us to "Come in and get geared up for the Red Wing Roots Music Festival," an annual summer bash in a rural spot we can't reach on foot, for which, the sign advises, we will need sunglasses and hats to protect us from the elements, hammocks for sleeping, headlamps to light our way in the dark between the electric, thumping stages, and sandals for dancing. We wish we could walk to the nearby hamlet of Singers Glen, named in honor of the music teacher and publisher Joseph Funk, whose singing schools established a tradition in the region, and whose shape-note hymnal, known as *Harmonia Sacra*, still draws groups together for a cappella singing.

Resonance Chamber

WHO WILL TRACE the echo to its source? The whole valley throbs with song. In musical instruments, a hollow resonance chamber amplifies soundwaves. As we reach our house at the bottom of the hill, we wonder if there is something conducive to the production of music in the local geography. Are these mountains the curves of a vast blue instrument? Do we live in a resonance chamber, cupped in a round, reverberant web of tones?

Dappled Things

EARLY IN THE MORNING, I walk to Hillendale Park. The sky is like gauze, with a pearly brilliance promising hot weather. Couples are out with their dogs, enjoying a stroll before it gets too warm; a jogger bounces over the gravel; an elderly walker overtakes me, moving with great energy, propelled by a pair of hiking poles. The park extends in three long stripes: meadow to my left, forest to my right, and the creek down the center. Blacks Run is shy here, hidden, identifiable only by its bridges, which arch over long, tufted grasses, as if the heat has transformed the creek from a body of water into a rustling, flaxen, threadlike material.

As I pass the familiar park structures—playground equipment, wooden pavilions with picnic tables—I consider the structure of the park itself, its pattern of grass and water and trees, its winding paths, the variety of its plants. Sun warms my left shoulder; my right is in the shade. The park has a dappled form, as if its planners set out to copy, on a large scale, the tracery of light and shadow that streaks the grass under the oaks, fluttering in a gust of wind.

Surely this is the most pleasant environment for walking: a shifting patchwork of brightness and dimness, a quilt of light.

Suddenly a deer walks up to the path. A beautiful little doe. She stops. I stop. For a moment we look at one another.

She is poised, neat and motionless, in the middle of the way. Then she turns, crossing unhurriedly to the forest side with lunging, almost turkey-like movements of her neck, with her reddish flanks and incredibly thin legs, the white and black of her tail. She has passed underneath the trees. She walks through the uneven drizzle of honeyed light that falls through the leaves, her little tail hanging darkly down. I start up the path again, perpendicular to her trail, watching her go, and she turns to look at me. Again she stops. I stop. She doesn't seem startled or afraid; she's just there, looking at me until she turns again to go, wandering into the shadows, becoming a small blurred ball of brownish stuff that vanishes in the deep green of the wood.

I know deer are considered a pest. They ravage gardens and cause traffic accidents. Once, when I was driving my son to soccer practice, a huge buck cantered out right in front of my car on Old Furnace Road, bearing antlers that looked to me, in my panicked state, about the size of my dining-room table. Fortunately, there was no one behind me, because without even glancing in the mirror, I slammed on the brakes. The buck crossed the road, then turned around and bounded across in the other direction, for all the world as if he owned the place. Deer, I admit, can be a menace. But how strange and marvelous it is when someone steps out of the trees and looks at you—someone of a different species with a pure, unfathomable gaze, like an animated particle of the forest.

The forest bears a trace of that enchantment. There's something solemn and magical about entering its shade. The summer growth has completely covered the dead leaves from last year, the whole floor is a leafy expanse lit by golden gleams of sunlight dripping down, and a sweetness fills the air, the rich smell of mold, of the old leaves crumbling into the earth, an intense distillation of decay and life, life and decay beneath this luxuriant growth, creeper and garlic mustard, pointy leaves, lobed leaves, heart-shaped leaves, oblong leaves, round leaves, jagged leaves, smooth leaves.

It's in the nature of variegated patterns to recede. Solid colors stand out; marbled colors are indefinite, fading into the background. Camouflage fabric is patchy, designed to disappear, like the deer in the wood or the creek in its cloak of weeds. These tiny flowers that stipple the forest floor—dainty yellow wood sorrel, fuzzy clover, smartweed strung with delicate amethyst beads—they're like the designs on decorative wallpaper, easy to ignore. It takes an effort even to see them (as well as, in my case, eyeglasses with the correct prescription). Yet how congenial, how restorative such surroundings are, these intricate tapestries that don't impose themselves on the eye, that don't seem to call for attention. Mottled patterns are forgettable because they enable a relaxed focus. To live in constant light or darkness would be a nightmare.

"Glory be to God for dappled things," Gerard Manley Hopkins says. The trees are thinning out ahead, the green light of the meadow growing stronger, and I draw in a few last ambrosial breaths of the cool of the wood, its loamy fragrance, and its subdued, beneficent, dappled atmosphere.

Night Walks

THE CITY BAKES under the heat dome. In the suffocating weather, we become night walkers, transferring our outdoor time to the hours of darkness. We go out at nine p.m. when the sun no longer burns, though the air is still close, heavy and enveloping like a fur. It's not quite dark. In the east, a few clouds are strung across the periwinkle sky, tipped with white or silver; in the west, the clouds are thicker, built up in opaque banks above the apricot band of the setting sun. We walk within a ring of clouds beneath the soft immensity of the sky. There is the evening star. Up the street, a little amber room shines out like a terrestrial star, with a picture on the wall and, in a basket on the windowsill, a sleeping cat.

    The pock of a pickleball echoes through the fence at the elementary school, mingled with louder slaps from the basketball court. Tall figures leap for the hoop; smaller ones watch, leaning on their bikes, or make their own game on the grass. The streetlamps begin to look brighter against the sky. At the same time, the fireflies come out, chips of yellow-green pulsing from the lawns. Kids still run and shriek in a few backyards, but the day is closing down, the life of the city absorbed into the houses. Peace descends on the porches, the rosebushes in bloom, and the open hillside leading up to the church with the arched, reddish-gold windows, its steeple faintly lit from below, the sky behind it smoky with outcroppings and curlicues of clouds suspended in the windless air.

In these long, curving residential streets, the distances become strange in the dusk. Sometimes a nervousness brushes over us in the wide gaps between the streetlamps—not a fear of violent crime, because it's common for people to walk alone in our city, even women and children, something for which we are grateful, and we know what we would do if we felt threatened, we'd run right up to a house, any lighted house, and knock at the door—so no, it's not fear that crisps our skin, just the alien feel of the darkness. It's the feeling that we can't quite trust our sight. We might pass a parked car and flinch as we suddenly realize there's a person inside it, a ghostly shape in the glass looking back at us, phone pressed to its ear. Objects are hard to recognize. A garden ornament or shrub might look like a dog in the gloom, a large unchained dog sitting in a yard. The big willow tree on Taliaferro Street, obliquely lit by a streetlamp, its trailing branches stirred by a stray breeze, becomes a mysterious troupe of cultists in green ceremonial robes performing a slow ritual dance on the grass.

This slightly unsettled feeling intensifies the cozy, intimate radiance of the lighted windows. We would like to assure our neighbors that we are not spying—we have no sinister designs—we simply love to see their windows lit up at night. Most of all, we love to glimpse a little corner of an interior, though we don't see many of those, since most people have their blinds down, their curtains drawn, just as we do at our house. The windows make luminous shapes along the street: the yellow of living-room lights, the bluish rectangles of television screens. Light filtered through curtains turns a whole room into a lamp. It's as if each curtain is a lampshade, the window bright as a bulb in the dark house. And how delightful it is when people suddenly appear: porch lights glinting down on couples sprawled on wicker couches, their hands raised in greeting as we pass, or a window with the blinds drawn up to reveal an old lady in a chair with several children playing around her. It makes us feel so snug, so tucked in, being out at night, seeing the silhouettes of plants in the windows, a foyer with a shelf full of porcelain figurines, a wall of framed, indistinct photographs. Why should we feel embraced when we're not in the house but walking along the street outside? It's a secretive, spellbound feeling, imagining the lives in the houses, spotting the beam of a desk lamp high in a curtainless room that makes us think of someone reading or writing. Somehow, when we see these interiors—people washing dishes or working on puzzles, big screens where video games are in progress, or one of those crowded rooms, all armoires, sideboards, and china cupboards, where lace doilies cover everything like snow—we imagine that the people inside are happy. Is this just our optimistic nature? Do other walkers imagine rooms full of sadness and distress? Or is there something inherently cheering about a lighted window, a domestic interior seen from the street?

Somebody's home. That's the feeling: Someone is there. Perhaps these lighted windows stir up childhood feelings, the memory of adult voices trailing down the street, the long singsong notes calling the children home.

Night thoughts in the night city. They swerve and stray, like our meandering path. The fireflies have snuffed their candles out. The overgrown yard on Green Street feels like a genuine forest in the dark, where nocturnal creatures leap and catch in our hair. The moon emerges from the mist, huge in the dark blue sky, irradiating the street that still gives off a hot tarry smell, and we wonder: Is the time coming soon when our city, like Miami, will have to hire a Chief Heat Officer? Passing the junglelike vacant lot where, earlier in the day, we glimpsed a tent half-concealed among the trees, we struggle in vain to make out its outline in the dark, wondering: Where would we go tonight if we had no home?

July

Softness

"Towns," writes the poet Anne Carson, "are the illusion that things hang together somehow." Today on Collicello Street, the illusion is particularly strong. Everything hangs together in an unbroken atmosphere of gentle wind and understated light, the houses grayish-white against a misty sky that seems to have absorbed the color of the tin roofs into its plush folds. Walking downtown is like plunging into a lukewarm bath, drifting south toward the blue-gray watercolor wash of the clouds, against which darker columns of vapor gather and fade. Turning east, I can count at least a dozen layers of cloud. Are they behind one another or on top of each other? The panorama of the sky keeps shifting, backlit by a silver glow. Its soft grayness infuses everything, even the green of the trees.

For more than ten years, I lived in deserts. I remember hard, stinging winds, gritty with sand and salt. There were steely breezes chilled by the ocean, hot drafts laden with dust, and suffocating gusts like the blast of a hairdryer. Here, there's no tension in the air. The flag on the grain elevator barely flutters, a small blot of rosy color between the purplish gray of the sky and the rabbit's-pelt gray of the tower. There's the greenish gray of a statue in a yard, a mossy boy and girl cuddling together. The thick gray of scaly porch steps, split to reveal a rotting interior. The clear, flawless gray of fresh siding. The pebbly gray of the asphalt, capturing the heat, sending tepid waves back into the grayness of the day.

Even the wind feels gray; it has the softness of a cat's back. It seems to come directly from the clouds—those feline clouds, white or gray with a hint of rainy blue, like the Russian blue cat I had years ago, or charcoal-colored like paw prints tracked across pale linoleum. In the cemetery, the wind pushes up against me just like a cat. It's big, forceful in its affection, but too soft to do any harm, this animal of heated air, eighty degrees at least, that has taken up residence among the gravestones, in the streets, all over the town.

For the Martinican philosopher Édouard Glissant, a certain kind of thinking was gray. He wrote about what he calls, in the translation of Betsy Wing, "the dove gray of thought." I'm drawn to this enigmatic image. How can thinking be gray, with the softness of a dove's throat? Glissant used this kind of thought to consider his landscape, tracing the sand and vegetation, lingering on a horizon "interwoven in variations of gray tinged blue with black, where space increases." It's as if his slowly probing philosophy found space to expand in the overcast, tropical atmosphere. The word Betsy Wing translates as "dove gray" is *grège*, which can mean raw silk or its subtle, uncertain color. Does soft, silken air, stirred by only the lightest, most caressing breeze, create a space for contemplation?

I'm tempted to say yes, circling among the slumbrous gardens of my city, passing the stately house on the corner, its silvery-gray turrets shading to white against the sky. I think of William Carlos Williams, who in *Paterson*, his love letter to his own town, wrote of "the green and dovegray countries of the mind." It's a fascinating coincidence—the way these two lyrical thinkers, Williams and Glissant, separated by time, space, and language, came up with such similar descriptions of a state of mind: an image of yielding dimness, intimately linked to an idea of space, to the act of writing about a landscape.

A humid stillness fills the valley with steam, swelling the wood of the houses, the juicy veins of the leaves. Is there a particular kind of thinking stimulated by such an atmosphere, an open, tentative philosophical attitude, like Glissant's? Perhaps this is going too far. After all, the deserts where I used to live are strongly associated with mental activity and the inner life. Since ancient times, prophets have retired to the desert to receive their visions. That stern, ascetic climate is the haunt of monks and mystics.

I wouldn't want to draw too firm a connection between an environment and the kinds of ideas produced there or the ways people live their lives. Yet I feel certain we are marked by landscapes. A town, it seems to me, is not only the illusion that things hang together but a genuine collaboration of things. Assembled and entangled, these things become more than the sum of their parts. They take on a collective energy. This might be what we mean when we say a city has a vibe, a personality, or even a heart.

Am I a different person now than I was when I lived in

the desert? There's something strange and a little disturbing about the idea of being shaped, independently of one's will, by geography. Yet how enticing it is, this feathered weather. In the incredibly long summer evening, the sun seems to be gradually disintegrating rather than setting, dropping its petals with infinite slowness. Streaks of fuchsia enter the cloud-hung sky. Fuzzy lamb's-ear grows densely near the curb, gray as celadon. I could happily melt into this lovely air, surrender to its influence, let my thoughts glide along its current, cradled by its fragrance of mown grass and the hint of petrichor, the odor of the earth after rain.

The Smallest House

IF YOU KNOW the Friendly City, you are familiar with its smallest house, tucked into an alley against the wall of a downtown restaurant. At the moment, the main features of this tiny domicile are a pair of gazebos (one crushed), a white picket fence, a front door, and a window with green shutters. I say "at the moment" because the smallest house has gone through a number of metamorphoses over the years. I have photographed it many times, like other passersby—those locals or students or traveling Civil War Trail enthusiasts you can find squatting in the alley, drawn to the city's minutest, most inexplicable attraction. I can remember when the wooden door was whole and uncracked, the fence smaller and unpainted, the mat adorned with the word *Welcome* surrounded by a woven design. There used to be a doll-size snow shovel leaning against the wall. A letterbox. A crate with gardening tools and itty-bitty seed packets. In those days, however, there was no window, no chalk portrait on the brick, and no gazebo, not even a broken one. The smallest house goes through periods of growth and decline, expansion and contraction, systole and diastole.

If you asked me to point out the physical location of the city's heart, I would place it here, not only because this alley cuts through the center of downtown, connecting the main parking garage with the courthouse, but because this is where you can take the collective pulse. The smallest house—humble, quirky, unprotected by official sanction or support, and exposed to passing feet in a busy walkway—offers an excellent measure of civic health. It's a good sign, I think, that so many people walk through here every day, zip past on skateboards and scooters, or stand about smoking or checking their phones, and the smallest house continues to exist. This diminutive artwork, so vulnerable to theft, defacement, and destruction, could not survive in a city with a meaner spirit.

Sensitive to changes in the temper of the town, the smallest house is the first place to show symptoms of communal weakness and decay. Earlier this year, around graduation time, somebody kicked it to pieces, almost obliterating it, wrecking the pink gazebo. But lo and behold, as if attended by industrious elves, the smallest house regenerated almost overnight. It even extended along the wall. A new fence appeared, a miniature cherry tree, a trio of bluebirds, a toy turtle holding a plastic bouquet.

This suggests that the Friendly City is not without flaws—we can be malicious, careless, or prey to an energy that turns aggressive. But we can also gather attention around a wounded spot. We can rebuild, and we can grow. I'm encouraged and uplifted every time I pass the smallest house, with its row of longsuffering plant pots, their green shoots torn away, its surprisingly hardy tree that seems to be made of some kind of playdough, its line of stones arranged into a wall.

I have heard that this fanciful public art installation is

the work of a local musician and performer, but surely the point of public art is that it belongs to the public. The smallest house is in our hands, given over to the community more fully than any municipal sculpture, as it's unauthorized, unfunded, and unsigned. It may have originated with one person, but others have contributed to its ongoing life. When I find a likely object on the street, I donate it to the house. I particularly recall a little plastic man I'd found in the gutter. Maybe you remember him—a sleek fellow in a gray suit, his arms crossed, his head turned to show off a profile adorned with a flamboyant mustache. He used to stand by the castle-like archway, where the toy turtle is now, near a plastic campfire where a cauldron presumably boiled his evening meal. A pale-green dragonfly hung out with him for a while. Then the man and the bug both disappeared. A pair of aliens replaced them, one with a strange dark jewel in its abdomen. After that came the bright-green, peg-like creatures in a flowered box labeled Goon Babies. Remember them?

Today I am adding a pair of new tenants: a tentacled gremlin of squishy pink plastic and a fuzzy green frog. The frog has a small metal loop on its head, as if it was once a child's pendant. The pink monster is hollow, like a finger puppet or a playful pencil ornament. I position them here in the heart of the city, against the bricks of a dignified building on the square, only a block away from the town's oldest extant structure, the mysterious Thomas Harrison House (mysterious because, according to archaeological evidence, the city's founder never lived there). The little frog has a few whitish patches where its green down has rubbed off. Will it be okay in the rain? I leave it behind, relinquishing it to the elements, to the city, thinking that this is only right, as I found it on the street, reflecting that the child who lost it might rediscover it here, and wondering, too, what an outsider would think of this gesture. I imagine a foreign anthropologist observing me from the corner, jotting down notes on the rituals of this place, recording how the inhabitants, as they traverse the alley, place small votive objects at the local shrine.

Developments

IN THE RELENTLESS HEAT, one thinks about the future. It's hard not to wonder where it's all going, what next summer will be like and the summer after that, walking down Washington Street in the hot, glazed afternoon toward the housing developments on the edge of town. On the hill, there's a prospect of shimmering shades that look tantalizingly cool: lush green trees, chalk-blue water tower, royal-blue mountains. Then you come down into the noise and swelter of things, the railroad tracks speckled with tough cornflowers, the auto body shops with their densely packed ranks of cars, the chatter of birds and radios. You can't see the mountains anymore.

Where the city thins out, the cars at the last mechanics' shops are parked in herds, as once cattle must have gathered in these fields. Outside a plain church with a blue door, an angel statue kneels with clasped hands. The sign on the lawn reads "Jesus Paid It All—You Keep the Change."

At the end of a long, lonely sidewalk, a development rises into view, townhomes painted the pale yellow of fresh butter. Identical wooden balconies throw grids of shadow across the back doors. In front, the units show a modest level of individuality, restricted to the same shape but using different colors and materials: sable brick with mint-green shutters, khaki siding with maroon shutters, biscuit-colored brick with dark-blue shutters. Across the street, another development presents a more uniform look, all tan walls, white balconies, and green trim. In the distance, the line of the mountains has resurfaced, a regular background against which the developments place their repetitive forms: the mailboxes for each section, the rows of satellite dishes, the grills on the matching patios.

There's a neatness to these complexes that feels a bit soulless to a passing stranger. The Friendly City's customary cheerful disorder is missing here, and the eye slides over the bricks and shutters longing for signs of personality, grasping gratefully at a pink bicycle or a doll with a missing leg. The place feels underdone, like dough that hasn't risen enough. It needs more time for the leaven of human presence to swell it up a little, nudging its edges out of shape. With the years, the flat colors of these houses will fade and fragment, until the development feels homey, crusty, and satisfying, baked to a warm golden-brown. Then the appearance of the place will harmonize with its general ambience, which is the atmosphere of a village, a sleepy hamlet where people know each other at least by sight and a visitor is a curiosity. Strolling through the development, you can feel interested glances flashing from the teenagers on a balcony and the woman washing her car. There's no reason to come to the development unless you live here or know someone here. The inhabitants eye you quizzically, but not at all coldly—rather, their gazes hesitate on the verge of welcome, as if you're about to become a neighbor or a friend.

You Keep the Change. Are these developments the future of the city? There are changes here that seem worth keeping. These townhomes represent what architects call the missing middle: buildings with multiple units that offer better walkability than apartment blocks and more efficient energy consumption than single-family homes. Popular until the 1940s, this type of clustered housing gave way to the detached, single-family style that characterizes much of the Friendly City, but it's returned to contemporary urban planning as a way to address housing needs, foster climate resilience, and keep cities alive.

As the Friendly City develops, these isolated housing estates may become more integrated into the town. Exiting the development, heading downhill, you pass the tienda—an encouraging sign, as a true missing-middle design should include a grocery store within walking distance. Farther on, there's a food truck by the side of the road, its little outdoor tables decorated with flowers. Maybe it will grow and be joined by other restaurants. You imagine the lawns of the developments transformed into community gardens, providing fresh vegetables to the tables of the future.

Circling toward home, you pass the Salvation Army, the family service center, and the emergency shelter. A crow paces in a parking lot, squawking frantically. You seem to be the only human being outside today. It's too hot. For most people, the distance you've walked this afternoon is too far, especially in this weather, but even on a beautiful day it takes too long, they have to get to work, to the post office, the health department, the daycare center, they've got small kids, too much to carry, so they drive their cars. In your imagined future city, people live closer to the places they need to go. Holding their children's hands, they cross the street. Bigger kids cycle on a network of paths, stopping to grab a few raspberries from the hedge. You can almost see them.

Sites of Memory

SHE SITS ON AN ISLAND between two streams of traffic, where Liberty Street and Main Street converge. Three flags rise above her. Bronze, sad-eyed, she spreads her arms in an open, compassionate posture, her head slightly bowed, pensive and resigned. Leaves of palm and laurel rest in her hands. A sword and rifle lean in the crook of her arm, pressing against the flowing folds of her dress. A soldier's helmet hangs from the scroll that unfurls from her right hand, on which forty-nine names are inscribed. The pedestal beneath her reads: "They tasted death in youth that liberty might grow old / 1917 World War 1918." As with many statues, her gaze has something mildly uncanny about it, sightless, unchanging. She is one hundred years old this month.

Her official title is *Liberty*, but the Friendly City knows her as Lady Liberty. Dark and graceful, she seems inked against the full summer green of the trees, the white streak of a church spire, and the smoky gouache of the sky. If you entered our town from the south, you might think this one image summed up the essence of the place: the war memorial, the church, the trees. The conjunction suggests a provincial spot with a somewhat defensive attitude, its focus turned inward toward its own small community concerns, its ventures in the outside world predominantly military.

In his richly illustrated book *Picturing Harrisonburg*—a monument in itself, which belongs in the library of any fan of the Friendly City—the historian David Ehrenpreis discusses the term "sites of memory." Such sites, which include historical landmarks and public statues like Lady Liberty, are "elements drawn from a community's past," he writes, "that take on symbolic importance and come to represent its values." Sites of memory are important for their ability to preserve a sense of history and develop collective relationships to place, but, Ehrenpreis warns, they never tell the whole story. His book is intended to explore "this gap between the real, lived experience and an imagined, aspirational ideal."

As I cross the street to the statue and climb the steps to its miniature garden, it's not the gap between the real and the ideal that preoccupies me but the strange dissonance within the image itself. How odd that the combination of this statue and a church steeple should create a closed and insular impression. You could just as easily see them as representations of the Friendly City's links to distant places and times. Lady Liberty's sandals and Greco-Roman drapery, the cross on the steeple—these are visual cues toward the cultures of the Mediterranean. One of the six African American dead mentioned on her memorial scroll is John Billhimer, who was buried in France. Of African ancestry, he lived an American life until the age of twenty-four; now his grave lies in Europe. By crystallizing a moment of the past, a site of memory can spark thoughts that range far beyond its surface simplicity, taking me from this garden of moss and heat-withered coneflowers to a sweeping historical arc that covers half the globe. And because I am a walker, I think also of other Friendly City walkers, of those who set out from our town a week ago, who are even now traveling on foot to the capital on a 135-mile antiwar protest march. A walk is in some ways the opposite of a monument: fluid rather than static, timebound rather than enduring. But this communal walk also shares certain qualities with a site of memory, as if such a site could be located in time instead of space. Like a physical monument, the walk takes on symbolic importance; it comes to represent the values of a community; it reflects the links between the local setting and the wider world; and it brings to light, painfully, in a meditation prolonged over many miles, the gap between the real and the ideal. Standing under the blank and sorrowful gaze of Lady Liberty, I think of the words of Ben Ridder, treasurer of the Dayton American Legion, the group that raised the statue—words often spoken, which have lost none of their force: "It was supposed to be the war to end all wars."

Memory is notoriously unpredictable at the individual level; it also shifts, David Ehrenpreis reminds us, at the collective level: "We continuously adapt and shape our own imaginings of the essential characteristics of a significant place." Walking home, I pass several sites of memory, identified by informational markers that gather tangled strands of history. There is the pillared municipal building that once, as the Confederate General Hospital, overflowed with the sick and wounded from two armies as the city rapidly changed hands. There is the quaint brick visitors center, once the home of the city's first mayor, where an enslaved woman named Fanny—one of our local history's most intriguing characters—used the food she earned as a Union Army cook to feed wounded Confederate soldiers, then left for freedom in General Sheridan's train. And there is, at the courthouse, the marker of the horrific lynching of Charlotte Harris. Sites of memory, sites of mourning, sites of speculation that send me searching, when I get home, for the biography of Charles Keck, the sculptor of Lady Liberty, discovering threads that link the Friendly City to other places touched by this artist's hand, such as nearby Charlottesville, where Keck made the statue of Stonewall Jackson that was removed from the city in 2021, and Rio de Janeiro, home of Keck's *Amicitia*, or Statue of Friendship, which the United States presented to Brazil as a centenary gift, and Brooklyn, New York, where the imposing façade of the Brooklyn Museum honors the wisdom of the world from ancient Greece to China, featuring sculptures representing Hebrew psalms, Persian philosophy, Indian literature, and Roman law, as well as Keck's contribution, *The Genius of Islam*.

Animal Encounters

RECENTLY, A NEIGHBOR told me, "I prefer our landscape of chickens and cows to all those horses and vineyards over the mountain."

A comment on wealth, on the contrast between the production of everyday staples and luxury items, and also on the feeling of a place. How a hillside changes depending on whether it's dotted with mild-eyed cows or statuesque horses. How rows of glistening grapes give off an exotic Tuscan light, so different from the dusty glow of chickens scratching in a yard.

This valley is poultry country, and in the Friendly City, chicken is king. Our most commanding architectural structures belong to the poultry plants; the railroad track is strewn with feathers and fallen grain, and trucks bearing crates of closely packed birds roll through town in a downy haze. Many city dwellers raise chickens on a small scale, for the eggs and the companionable presence of these plump, mincing creatures, who enliven our neighborhoods with the nervous gaze of their ancient dinosaur eyes and the sound of their monotonous, fussy clucking.

Humble, domestic, and of a nice, manageable size, the chicken is a good representative of the city's animal kingdom. Our beasts are on the small side, built to scoot out of sight underneath a car if necessary. Squirrels, rabbits, possums, groundhogs, raccoons, and mice populate our yards, fluctuating with the time of year, along with the cardinals, robins, and other petite birds that fill the air with song, watched by a multitude of regal, bored-looking cats. The largest of the urban fauna are occasional deer and ubiquitous dogs. The latter, while beloved members of many households, are also the most likely to provoke a passing walker. I have often inched warily past a yard where an untied dog barked at me in alarm, both of us calmed only by the presence of the smiling pet owner on the porch.

Seasonal visitors add a particular spice to walks in the city, combining the excitement of change with the satisfying familiarity of return. The ducks of the creek come so regularly they have recently been celebrated in a series of statues scattered through downtown. Canada geese descend on the ponds of the state university in the warmer months, along with families of shy turtles, whose young, compact and gleaming like agate marbles, can be seen sunning themselves on a muddy pipe that juts out over the water.

There is a season of field crickets, a season of garter snakes, a season of spiders. Many porch ceilings are painted haint blue to ward off malevolent spirits and/or wasps. We are entangled, even in the city, with what the philosopher David Abram calls the more-than-human world. And since this is an urban space edged with the rural, where a ten-minute drive in any direction takes you into the country, the Friendly City has a close relationship with farmland, visible in the local businesses selling agricultural equipment, the tractors that occasionally slow the traffic, and the livestock auction just over the hill from my house. Tales are told in my neighborhood of escaped pigs being chased through the streets and the dramatic execution, some years ago, of a wayward bull. Country and city are woven together, taking part in each other's lives. In my household, we are urban folks, but our uncle once kept a small dairy nearby, our cousins sell pork and poultry at the weekly farmers market, and visits to friends often take us to porches where cows watch us blandly over the fence.

How the creatures of the Friendly City have enriched my walks with their presence, like stars in the night sky! The deer in the park. The crow on a wire, balanced so neatly in its black leather tailcoat. The large brown snake I watched in the creek near the Ice House, whipping itself upstream with a startling jackknife motion. The rabbit washing its face and long ears with such feline movements I have thought of the species, ever since, as a type of skittish, vegetarian cat. The bashful groundhog that played peekaboo with me under a bridge. The curious turtle that stretched its neck toward me, wrinkled and imperious, like a cantankerous professor. And even the dog that tyrannized my neighborhood for a year.

He was a terrier, small in stature but huge in personality, whose proud throat had never known either collar or chain. During his reign, the portion of the street claimed by this irascible animal took on the menacing air of a mountain pass haunted by highway robbers. Every time I passed the place—

which unfortunately lay between my house and my job—a wild ball of fur with needle teeth hurled itself at me, bristling with rage and baying for my blood. This dauntless dog attacked pedestrians and cyclists with equal ferocity. Eventually, he even tussled with a car, which we thought would mean his end, but like Billy the Kid, the legendary gunslinger he so resembled, he had a matchless power to defy the laws of both man and nature. After being hit by the car, he returned to his post, madder than ever and sporting a rakish new haircut like a badge of honor. He long evaded punishment, continuing to terrorize the street even after he'd bitten two kids and an animal control officer. At last he was apprehended, but he left behind, as a lasting memorial on the house he once guarded with such unrestrained devotion, a scar tissue of scratches and holes in the front storm window, evidence of his audacious plan to bite his way through the plastic.

I do not miss this dog. But the thought of his mischief reminds me that the more-than-human world does not always play by human rules, and that while life with the local critters is full of wonder and affection, it's also often scrappy, uncomfortable, and tragic. Above all, it's unpredictable—but isn't this where stories come from? Since moving to the Friendly City, we have met several people who have been swarmed by yellowjackets, one who was bitten by a copperhead (her unflappable parents told her to take an aspirin and go to bed), and another who broke a rib when he fell down while chasing a rooster.

August

Dear Neighbor

Dear Neighbor,

I wonder if you know how much I like walking by your house. Your house on the corner, so low, just one story, beneath enormous leaning trees, with your worn porch furniture and the lumpy bed for the dog to lie on. Your house midway up the street, the arched windows all filled in with concrete and fronted with iron spikes like a medieval cloister. Your house in the elegant neighborhood where you've allowed your yard to run riot and dust to darken your impressive old windows. Your house in the modest neighborhood where you've painted your front door orange and bordered the sidewalk with sunflowers. All your houses, neighbor.

Tonight I walked past your house and you waved to me from the porch so cheerily it felt like you were glad to see me again, although we've never spoken. I walked past your house and you were washing a bunch of plastic basins in the front yard and one of your kids was running around naked. You were standing on a ladder, nailing something to the porch. Half concealed behind the heat-crisped dogwood, you were having a quiet phone conversation in Spanish. You'd set up a row of lawn chairs, their legs sunken in the grass, and brought a screen and projector outside, and your kids were all excitedly watching a cartoon that lit up the dark street with a green light, while you and the other adults passed to and fro with drinks. You were just coming home, opening your front door, a bearded stranger, and I glimpsed the string bass leaning against your living-room wall. Neighbor, it was awesome to think of you playing that thing in the evenings for the dog that was pushing past you into the house.

Your house always looks so eerie and withdrawn when I come down the hill past your severe dry lawn, where no tree or shrub grows. The two cars are always parked under the shelter, the rooms shrouded in darkness except for the single light in an upstairs window. I've got no idea what's going on in there, whether you're ill or just resting or thinking, why nobody ever seems to go in or out. But when I see these familiar signs, when I sense your special aura of seclusion, I know you're still there. Year after year, I pass the reassuring evidence of your ongoing presence, neighbor. Those rusty bicycle wheels hanging up in your porch—they couldn't belong to anyone else. Who else would leave the front window clogged with an impenetrable curtain of ivy, or build those teetering towers of luggage in the screened-in porch? Meandering through town, I note your boarded-up attic window, your purple awning, your gray-and-white cat limp as a washrag on the front step, ticking them off in my mind almost ritualistically, the way, as a child, I used to count the banister rails when running down the stairs.

How can I say this without overstepping the bounds of propriety? I feel like your house is my house. No, I wouldn't go inside without being invited, or even cross your lawn, but your home is part of my habitat. Feelings are not bound by property lines. When I walk out my front door, my path flows across my porch and down the steps to a sidewalk that leads me straight into your geraniums. Sometimes I feel like the whole portion of the city I can reach on foot is a busy, checkered extension of my house. The word *habitat* comes from the Latin verb *habitare*, a frequentative form of the verb *habere*, which means to have or hold. Habitation is an intense and repetitive form of having. What's the difference between walking from my kitchen to my living room and from my front porch to yours? It's just a longer walk.

Do you feel the same way about my house? The walls we painted coral, the porch where the cushions are perpetually falling off the swing, the chaos of herbs and weeds in the front yard, and the headstrong, anarchic redbud?

Tonight I walked past your house and all your belladonna lilies were in bloom. They stood upright in your yard, frail and vital at once, their color rising like mist in the dusk, turning the whole street pink. I thought of the care you had taken to plant these flowers that would bloom for such a short time before being withered by the heat and flattened by storms. And I hoped you would stay around for a long time, neighbor, with your flowers and motorcycles, your bushes and boxes, your trellises and broken cars, your wind chimes and outdated campaign posters and dog bowls and beds of kale that constitute my habitat, and without which I would not recognize my home.

Enchanted Forest

"Have you ever walked in the Enchanted Forest? It's a delight!"

Cross Maryland Avenue where the scaffolding of the electric station scribbles gray lines against the sky. Stop to peer down at the creek flowing under the road, brown and shallow, overhung with trees and jammed with fallen branches. Walk up the grass toward the school. The trees rise in somber ranks, making a sharp line against the sloping lawn. A duck waddles out of your way, her drab flank adorned with a single iridescent feather like an heirloom of blue glass.

No, I told my friend, I'd never been there. I thought I'd walked everywhere I could in this town, circled every place I could reach from my front door. It was during the COVID-19 pandemic that I really became a walker, taking long rambles just for something to do. I rapidly tired of treading the same ground and began charging off in different directions, plunging down side streets in search of variety. But somehow I never came to the forest at the elementary school, though it wasn't an enchanted forest at the time, just an overgrown knot of trees, the old trails clogged and impassable. I never realized there was a forest here.

A hawk flies over the treetops with a sharp, mewing call. Starry thistles and pink knobs of pokeweed embroider the edge of the wood. When you step in under the trees, the air turns emerald. It's close and hot in here on a summer day, but there's relief from the sun. A sign beside the leaf-fringed, light-dappled trail points the way to the Fairy Forest: *El Bosque de Hadas*.

When you think you've walked every inch of the Friendly City, it seems there's always another corner, a hidden angle, the hills shifting in kaleidoscopic fashion, unfolding unexpected colored planes, fresh squares of light and darkness, secret nooks and hollows.

The forest is full of sound. When you enter its shadows, you're immersed in its soundscape, which makes it feel like a different world. Cicadas shrill their single maniacal note. Birds chime in: raucous jays, liquid-throated cardinals, whistling finches, robins yapping like puppies. There's something you can't identify—an insect, a bird, a frog?—that sounds like a rusty doorknob being turned over and over. Deep among the trees, where much of this noisy life is hidden, it seems as if the wood itself is singing.

The forest features a prettily carved "hobbit door" entrance, inspired by the writer J. R. R. Tolkien, who had a passion for enchantment. Enchantment, he used to say, is different from magic. Magic is an illusion, like a coin trick that makes a quarter seem to disappear when in fact it's concealed inside a palm. Enchantment creates the dream of another world, one we can enter, coming face to face with wonder. Tolkien considered enchantment a fundamentally healing experience, which revives our relationship with the world, providing "a clear view." Jaded adults need this a lot more than children do. "We should look at green again," he wrote, "and be startled anew."

After several twists and turns, you enter the clearing of the Stump School, where the little people have been at work. Twisted branches make a fort. Stumps stand in rows before a chalkboard. A tapestry hangs unfinished on a loom. The place has a strangely inhabited air, though no one's around at this hour. It's as if the shy denizens of this glade have just tiptoed away—perhaps to curdle somebody's milk or tie knots in a horse's mane. You almost expect to hear a chuckle from the undergrowth.

I think the Enchanted Forest must feel like another world to the children who come here. Although it's not a big wood—a grown walker will quickly loop through its network of paths—its bowery darkness makes a striking contrast with the clear, open lawns of the play areas and the brightly lit world of school. How fun it must be to have class outside, perched on chunks of wood like elves in a storybook! If these children return to the Enchanted Forest after a space of years, I imagine, they'll laugh with surprise at how small it is, as a person can be startled, on a visit home, by the absurdly cramped dimensions of a childhood bedroom.

A lone cabbage white flits among the ivy like an animated shred of paper. A series of steps overrun with vines leads down into the foliage. Cypresses, roughly chopped back, stand with their reddish bark exposed. And a giant mulberry tree—weary-looking, apparently half dead, trailing appendages like strange long fingers—gives you a wise, arresting glance from its single wrinkled eye. This must be the guardian of the wood.

For grown folks, too, this shady grove may hold a spark of charm—what my friend called *delight*. As I conclude my visit, emerging from the trees onto the grass that leads down to the road, I think of Tolkien's walking song—a poem about traveling on foot through unknown lands, setting off in untried directions into the veiled, ever-beckoning depths of a landscape.

> *Still round the corner there may wait*
> *A new road or a secret gate,*
> *And though we pass them by today,*
> *Tomorrow we may come this way*
> *And take the hidden paths that run*
> *Towards the Moon or to the Sun.*

This Path Is Not for You

Friends and neighbors, I advise you not to walk on Country Club Road.

My plan is simple: I've decided to walk from the synagogue to the nearby mosque, an easy twenty-minute stroll according to my GPS. It seems right that these houses of worship should stand just a mile apart, since the Friendly City's Jewish and Muslim communities often cooperate with one another (a partnership that has continued during this devastating year). I start at the synagogue, a short walk from downtown, taking a moment to circle the Jewish cemetery, where tall pines cast their shadows over the headstones, and sit on a bench in this enclosure, which preserves a hush despite the traffic passing beyond the low stone wall. When clouds cover the sun, the light-green moss on the ground shines out of the gloom. The trees hold up their tasseled arms, their crowned heads, against the towering rain-filled clouds and a sky that seems refreshed, its blue rinsed clean by the cooler weather over the last few days. There is a tenderness to this cemetery, so small, with the little stones laid on the grave markers, along with other tokens of remembrance: a stained-glass dove, a ceramic map of Virginia on a leather strap, a seashell. Around the corner stands the synagogue, a brick building bearing a sign that reads "This is My name for ever and this is My memorial unto all generations." The breeze rises as I turn and walk down Market Street, past the Budget Inn, toward the mosque, toward the mountains.

The trouble begins on Vine Street. Here the sidewalk disappears. There's no crosswalk where I have to cross the street onto Country Club Road, but I manage to dash through a gap in the traffic and gain the safety of the Chamber of Commerce, where I stop to catch my breath on the lawn. Our Chamber of Commerce is an attractive house with a row of dormer windows, but I don't advise you to walk there! I'm just glad it's a public building, because I am tramping over the grass so as not to risk getting hit by the stream of vehicles rounding the corner. Here's a yard sale offering stuffed animals and autumn-themed decorations; I don't want to buy anything, but I gladly take the opportunity to walk through the yard. Here's a pretty little church, its white doors bright against the brick. I hope the congregants carpool or have set up some kind of shuttle service! As for me, I'm in somebody's driveway right now, because there's nowhere to walk. I'm in someone's yard, trudging through clover, burrs, and bees.

Have you ever been driving through the Friendly City, relaxed at the wheel, listening to your music, absently running through your to-do list in your head, when you realize with a shock that you've narrowly missed running over some dimwit who is inching along the trees by the side of the road? Neighbor, that moron might have been me. In my defense, I didn't know the sidewalk was going to vanish. I didn't expect to be spilled onto a road that is clearly meant only for cars, plunked down on a strip of grass littered with cups and cigarette packets, pressed up against the rough, prickly trees.

Look—don't do this. Do not try to walk on Country Club Road. There are no more houses here, no helpful yards or driveways. The traffic comes whipping around the curves; there's no chance for the drivers to see me before they're on top of me. I stumble over tin cans, cardboard hamburger containers, the rubbery lid of a cooler, and other junk people have thrown out of their cars. The branches of these bushes, whatever they are, are covered with needle-sharp thorns that stab my hands as I try to protect my face. Sometimes the impenetrable vegetation forces me onto the road, and I wait, peering from the thicket, trembling like the terrified forest creature I've become, for a break in the traffic that lets me skitter out onto the tarmac, then dive back to be impaled on the thorns before the next car comes.

As a bonus, a cyclist hurtles past within an inch of my ear! For yes, there is a bike lane on Country Club Road—a frankly laughable stripe of white paint, along which an extremely thin cyclist on a streamlined machine might just squeak through. The biker barrels past me, eyebrows raised in surprise and teeth showing, unbelievably, in a genial smile. "Hi!" he exclaims, when he ought to be screaming at me to get out of the way, as his other side is being menaced by a Honda. It's times like these that make me think we really do live in the world's friendliest town. But I also suspect I've just encountered a serious thrill seeker—a guy who's decided to bike this route for the pleasure of taking his life in his hands, and whose fun would only be enhanced if a bear were set loose in the road. What's a pedestrian to him? I imagine him describing our meeting to friends later—probably drinking a beer, seated at the very edge of his roof—and laughing over the scratched, horrorstruck face of the lady he passed in the weeds, who was clearly too panicked to say hello.

And then there it is: the mosque, rising serenely into the sky, its yellow wall gleaming against beds of orange and carmine flowers. Sunlight warms the coppery dome, the sparkling brass crescents, and the pinkish-brown surface of the minaret, so highly polished it looks enameled. This graceful building exudes an air of stillness, as if some invisible barrier separates it from the noise of the road. A sense of reprieve, of retreat, links it to the synagogue and the little cemetery a mile away—although, as I've learned, for a walker they are not as close as they seem.

On my way home, seeking a saner route, I manage to avoid a stretch of Country Club Road by taking Clay Street. But from what I can tell, there is no fully safe and enjoyable way to walk from the synagogue to the mosque. If the local Muslim and Jewish communities have a history of collaboration, it's not because of the cityscape but in spite of it. They have had to make plans and spend gas money; there is no possibility of a casual amble into one another's spaces, of simply dropping by. I'm left with the memory of a discarded sign, a relic from some unknown social event, glimpsed among the litter in the grass along Country Club Road, its imagery featuring an optimistic pink thumbs-up cartoon, its text welcoming the public in seven languages.

Why Here?

"I have a question for you," he said. "Why do you live here?"

He was young, and had lived in the Friendly City for about four years. He went to college here and graduated this past spring. He smiled as he asked the question, but his gaze was uncertain, even a little desperate. I imagined that as the city filled up with college students again, those migratory birds that land in huge flocks every autumn, he was wondering why he was still hanging around this undistinguished spot, why he hadn't moved on.

And did he have to leave? Or was this a reasonable place to live—as good as any other?

I smiled back at him and went into my usual recitation: I applied for a job here because I have friends and family in the area; I grew up visiting the town; I like the four seasons, the mountains, the proximity to larger cities. I could tell from his polite nod and suppressed sigh that he wasn't satisfied. What surprised me was that I wasn't convinced myself. Everything I said was true, but it was so vague as to have little meaning. When I walk through town, when my step quickens with sudden happiness, it's not because I'm thinking about my job, my friends, the nearness of the capital city, or even the mountains.

What is it, then?

It's the towering plaster rooster in a garden, overshadowing a statue of a small boy in gray stone.

It's the house at the top of the hill completely surrounded by children's playhouses, as if a miniature tribe has besieged and conquered the adults.

It's the three plastic horses in a yard, each about two feet high, one of them painted a wonderful delicate raspberry color, who seem ready to gallop into the yellow scrub behind the house, their diminutive size transforming it into a field of waving golden grass.

It's the statue of a stag balanced on a ceramic turtle.

It's the big rusty ogre, taller than a man, who guards a certain backyard, a creature composed of some bubbly substance I can't identify, similar to papier-mâché but impervious to rain. It's his mighty, purplish head, which I saw lying on the front porch the other day, removed (temporarily, I hope) for some kind of surgical procedure. It's the fact that this monster exists nowhere else. His DIY eccentricity. The ambition behind his construction, the humor, the verve.

It's the row of modest houses painted in light, unobtrusive colors, each with a demure green patch of yard, and the fact that one of these yards contains an enormous skeleton, its skull almost level with the upstairs windows. Maybe this ghoul started out as a Halloween decoration, but it's become part of the street, winter and summer. I love the weird silhouette of its long, creaky limbs, its jaws grinning through the branches of a pear tree, and, even more, the tolerance of its neighbors, the way nobody on this otherwise normal block seems to be asking questions about the oversized cadaver. One feels that although the neighbors may disapprove of this gaunt totem, may even grumble about it, clicking their tongues irritably as they peer through the curtains, they would all staunchly defend their neighbor's right to self-expression, and if the skeleton were threatened by outsiders, they'd rise to its defense.

It's the giant frog on a porch railing. The cow skull on a door. The sculpture of a surprised-looking boy riding on a pterodactyl. These rough-and-ready arts, these distinctive combinations of objects offered to the gaze of passersby, to the street.

It's the porch with the silver mannequin torso, the green rabbit, the purple cat in a face mask, the blue chicken, the plaster head of a Roman centurion, the bug-eyed alien resting on its elbow, the colorful plastic replica of a sugar skull, and the dented robot cobbled together from spare parts. This porch is a little vision of utopia. If a rabbit can hang out with a robot, it suggests, and a soldier of the ancient world can rub shoulders with a creature from outer space, then there is room for everyone here.

It's the carousel horse in a glassed-in porch, leaning against the wall, looking far too large for the space, exiled from the fairground of its youth, and the way the lamps in the garden shine up onto its red-and-blue trappings after dark, transforming it into a figure of romance.

It's the place on Grace Street where the creek flows under a university building—yes, they put a building on top of the creek!—and the tarry-looking water goes sliding along on its secret way, and in summer there's a loud, chittering echo from below, as if birds are fighting or holding a parliament in the culvert, and you can hear the water pouring over stones and bricks and rust-bitten pieces of pipe, and the bank is all overgrown, and there's lots of graffiti on the wall, so it must be easy to climb down there, and someone has painted a little green dragon sticking out its long tongue, or possibly vomiting, and shouting "Blargh!"—or, again, perhaps this "Blargh!" is the sound of dragonish regurgitation—and turning up its eyes, and stiffening its ridiculous stubby arms, and the effect is comical and sly and a bit disruptive in a high-spirited way, without malice, with the air of something done for a lark, from sheer exuberance, and I realize this might be an odd reason to love a place, but there's something so charming about this zaniness and greenness tucked away beneath the street, this conjunction of leaves and water and stone and a sense of the absurd that seems to ask, with merry philosophy, Why not here?

September

Everyday Losses

"I REMEMBER so many places," she says, "that aren't here anymore."

I often think of her when I walk past the bus shelter on Grace Street, which doubles as a historical marker, with its large photograph of the Rockingham Cooperative Farm Bureau complex that stood here from 1932 to 2013. A parking deck now occupies the site. I think of how she must have taken this same walk, when she was a child, to go downtown, and how different it must have felt, how the noises and smells of the street have changed, and even the quality of the light. Sitting with her in a coffee shop, listening to her stories, I have a strange sensation of doubling: the feeling of contrasting time periods layered onto the same space, as the photograph at the bus stop is lined by the masonry behind it and scrawled over by scratches in the plastic wall.

Every Saturday, she tells me, she and her sister would walk downtown for their piano lesson at the Miles Music building on Mason Street. She was nine years old and her sister was seven. After their lesson, they'd go to the Peoples Drug Store on Main Street for a sandwich at the lunch counter. They always ordered the same sandwiches—one grilled cheese and one ham—and traded halves. "It was great," she says, "because eventually the women behind the counter just knew who we were." Then they'd walk home down Water Street, past the old jail, and stop in at Novelty News to get the latest *Archie* comics. She and her sister would each choose one, and then they'd sneak to the back of the place and try to glance at the *Playboy* magazines, and inevitably the man at the register would holler, "Okay, you kids! Come on!" Later, she says, when they were teenagers, they'd go to Novelty News for Swisher Sweets cigars, which made them sick.

On Liberty Street, they'd stop at the Ice House and stand in front of the big doors, which were always open, to feel the cold pouring out and watch the men working with the ice in their thick coats, breathing out heavy plumes of fog. She remembers how the jail moved around, and how it grew, gobbling more and more space, until the jail and courthouse took over a whole block, pushing out all the businesses there, the fine old bars she remembers and the Ole Virginia Ham Café, an enormous place with wonderful homemade food. And oh, the amazing chicken salad and strawberry shortcake at the Downtown Café! A certain flavor, which once characterized this place, has slipped away, wafting into history with the fragrance of a particular cake, fading along with the deep glow of the carpet at the Virginia Theater.

She remembers the grandeur of that theater on Main Street, which had once been an opera house and a venue for vaudeville shows. "It was done in the old style," she says: an elegant lobby, a beautiful theater, an orchestra pit with an organ, red velvet curtains on the stage. A long carpeted ramp led up from the street level to the lobby. And there was another hallway, she says, her eyes gleaming, going down to the left, which got darker and darker and ended at the Arcade. There was a bowling alley back there, she remembers, pool tables, a bar, and naughty magazines and postcards for sale. Once, as a child, she followed her older brother into the Arcade and a man immediately came up to her, took her by the shoulders, turned her around, and sent her out the door. "I'll never forget it!" she says, laughing.

They tore down the Virginia Theater and put in a parking lot. But you can still see, she tells me, in the brick buildings downtown, the outlines of former architecture, the shadowy shapes of windows that will never open again.

It's not entirely a case of mourning the past. She loves the Friendly City today, especially its diverse culture, the many languages spoken here, the varieties of music and food. And there are some places from the past she doesn't miss, like the downtown biker bar she would always cross the street to avoid, a place seething with fights and drunken mayhem—though even here she can't help giggling with delight over the name of the place: Eddie's Broken Spoke. No, it's not that one doesn't want things to change—change is unavoidable in cities, as more generally in life, and often necessary and welcome. But who, having known it, can forget the peculiar aura of drama and dilapidation that surrounded Eddie's Broken Spoke? How can she pass the café on the corner without thinking of the Friendly City's first head shop? Once, it filled this space with its black light posters and beaded curtains. She could never purchase anything incriminating, she remembers with a grin, because her friend's mother worked there. "That's where I bought my first pair of jeans."

Places have an afterlife. Their images are carried in the memories of people who pass, every day, the new objects and structures that have replaced the old. And since a city is made of people as well as places, it works like a palimpsest, traces of ancient script showing through the writing of today.

As we set down our empty cups and prepare to say goodbye, we talk about the old Red Front grocery store—a place I've lived here long enough to remember—and the sadness of its blank windows and funereal, abandoned parking lot. I deeply miss this place, which shut down four years ago. The fact that there was once an affordable independent grocery store in my neighborhood already feels legendary. As I part from my friend with a hug, it occurs to me that such losses are an inevitable consequence of belonging to a place. If you pass certain street corners with a pang, if ghosts gesture from boarded-up windows, it's because you've lived in that place long enough to see it change.

Recently, someone told me that Red Front is going to be turned into a nightclub. Can this be true? I imagine the old store persisting, phantomlike, beneath the new establishment: strains of the grocery's light Christian rock seeping through the dance beats; between the dancers, racks of those Amish romance novels known as bonnet rippers; and, rising spectrally behind the bar, tubs of brilliantine and towering, church-picnic-size jars of pickled red beet eggs.

Second Spring

THE PERFECTION, the absolute perfection of a golden September day in the Friendly City.

An alertness, a subtle liveliness is infiltrating the air. Early in the morning, pink clouds glisten in a sky brushed with layers of blue lacquer. As the light grows, the clouds lose their blush, turning into wandering isles of radiant whiteness, with sharply defined shadows like forests on their flanks, drifting across a sea of sky.

For a few days, there were hints of what was coming. You could feel it in the freshness of the air, the coolness of your evening walks. You put on a long-sleeved shirt. And now what was approaching has arrived: slender breeze, warm sun, no humidity, and pure, bright light on this house where paper bags are hanging up on the porch, maybe to dry herbs, you imagine, or ward off wasps. And the creek, which looked so cloudy and strange last week—a motionless, milky olive green, as if detergent had been dumped in it—is running brown and transparent, revealing the edge of every stone. The water has become as clear as the sky.

Pallid hydrangeas touched with red, as if dusted with cinnamon sugar.

Gossamer on the trees. Deep pools of shade at the foot of the hill. It's as if summer is turning over in its bed, settling itself, exposing a silvery flicker of its autumn blanket, then turning again, heating up, half waking, because certainly there will be more hot days before the season changes, but the summer is unmistakably growing drowsy, snuggling down, preparing to drop off under a heap of fallen leaves.

A buttery glow suffuses the old house across the street, coating the rusty roof with a precious amber gloss.

Two mushrooms in a grassy yard reflect the light with a stout, martial glare, like a pair of brass buttons.

Cosmos flowers riot in the gardens, their color recalling a certain firm, vivid, almost piercing yellow-orange crayon you used as a child to draw the sun. On the square, petunias emblazon the sidewalks, echoing the rainbow of the Love sign left over from the recent Pride celebrations.

A burst of blooms. A flourishing of color that seems to be pressed urgently out of the plants, like a cardinal's song from its throat. As if something is saying: Now, before it's too late. Now, the fleshy sunflowers nodding over the top of a wall, the great yawning hollyhocks in their almost criminal crimson, the ragged extravagance of the chenille with its flowers like fat red pipe cleaners, the amaranths in clumps of fiery coals. Now, the zinnias in auburn and cherry pink, the dahlias bearing their crinkled globes like paper lanterns, the butterfly bush with its purple spires of incense. And everywhere, now, now, the crape myrtle laden with its burgundy, ruby, or lavender burden.

So many flowers are yellow, pink, or red, the streets of the city seem bordered with a steady flame. Cockscombs unfurl the stiff, almost shocking claret brilliance of their fans. Scarlet trumpet vines clamber over a fence, while down below, the humble pumpkin flower contributes the weathered yellow of old gardening gloves.

But as if to protest, to insist that the warm-toned flowers will not have the season all to themselves, chicory winks along the sidewalk with winsome blue eyes, morning glory drapes its cobalt mantle over a hedge, and the balloon flower explodes into a veined violet star.

There are white flowers, too, that splash the streets with foam. The white crape myrtle and butterfly bushes stand like brides among their florid sisters. Ivory garlic chives flower in kitchen gardens. And all along this rustic alley, smothering the wall, the autumn clematis pours out effervescent constellations with the mouthwatering aroma of waffles and syrup.

If you dropped down suddenly into this place without knowing the time of year, you might think it was spring. But then the fading roses would give the season away, here at the corner where they offer their last, sad, eau-de-cologne scent, some still faintly pink, but most already sallow, drooping, clotted like peach cobbler, the lower branches withered into antique lace.

Between the throbbing summer and this cooler, spring-like season, there was a bridge of rain. I remember, after a sudden shower, watching three children run barefoot along the gutter, kicking up the coral petals of the crape myrtle that had blown down during the storm—flowers so abundant they blocked the drain, spreading out in lakes of rosy silk trimmings, tumbling down the hill to pile up at a bend in the street in evanescent banks of cotton candy.

The stillness of the morning. Shrill, incessant birds and insects. And what is that exquisite fragrance on the air? That elusive, woody, invigorating scent—is it soil? Is it just the dew on the grass? Is it autumn?

The Other Side

IN THE 1930s, the German Jewish writer Siegfried Kracauer fled the Nazis to Paris. He fell in love with the city's neighborhoods, especially the disorganized and seedy ones, where, he wrote, he would walk for hours, captivated by "the intoxication of the streets." These labyrinthine streets felt organic to him, "like the limbs of living things." Deep in their crevices, he felt as if he were searching for some lost destination or memory. "Filled with the longing to finally reach the place where what I'd forgotten would come back to me, I could not pass the smallest side street without entering it and turning the corner at its end."

Today I'm walking through the lanes behind Liberty Street, not as a shortcut to anywhere, not because there's anything in particular to see back here, but simply because, like Kracauer in Paris, I cannot pass the smallest side street without entering it and turning the corner at its end. Behind the big old homes that have been converted into student housing, smaller structures stand pressed together in lines. I assume they're inhabited by students too, until I pass a very old man standing by a mailbox, apparently lost in thought. I weave among these apartments, crossing their parking lots, their strips of grass, the shadows of their rickety balconies, entering an alley where a fake deer gazes soulfully at me from a yard as if mourning its lost plastic forest. Here's a boat swathed in a dusty tarp, a firepit made of loose bricks, a kayak on a porch, a railing crowded with bicycles. I've passed these houses before, but now I'm seeing them from the back, from the other side of the tapestry, where seams and stray threads show.

When you walk in a limited space, there are two ways to experience newness. You can observe how the landscape changes (seasons shift, people move in and out, the creek runs high or low), or you can take matters into your own hands, wriggling onto the other side, discovering novel angles on familiar things. My walks are constrained by ability and time, as I always start from the same place—my front porch—and go as far as my legs and schedule allow, usually not more than a few miles, an hour and a half at most. So I often try to get onto the other side, preferring the crooked road to the straight, the cluttered alley to the open sidewalk, and even the dead-end street to the more promising thoroughfare.

In the Friendly City, it's worth noting, a dead end is not always dead to a pedestrian. I cut through a stretch of weeds beside the creek, climb up to the bridge, and pick my way across the railroad track to enter the back of the lumberyard. I experience the good cheer that always fills me when I've managed to walk somewhere I couldn't drive or even bike. Here, on the flip side of the tapestry, the city feels raw and ragged: motionless train cars, dark as mahogany with age and exposure, stand as if glued to the tracks; planks lie piled in the parking lot; scrawls of graffiti cover the outbuildings like colorful tangles of yarn. It is not, perhaps, to everyone's taste to walk through a lumberyard, but I love to see how the city is put together, to trace the knots. And if I never strayed from the most obvious paths, I wouldn't be facing, right now, the gorgeous stained glass in the house that suddenly looms up at the end of the street, catching the sun with its circlets of molten gold, purple diamond panes, and opalescent squares like mother-of-pearl.

Once, while searching for a place to lock up my bicycle at the Family Dollar on Chicago Avenue, I found myself overlooking a patch of countryside bordered by a small vegetable garden and a field of corn. A forest adjoined this rural scene. How strange to realize I was looking at the back of the bike path—a route I've walked and biked hundreds of times! The forest was the thicket of trees along the path, the corn was growing in someone's backyard, and the vegetable garden belonged to the auto body shop whose roof, scattered with tires, lay below my vantage point. In all my roaming through this neighborhood, I had never before discovered that these enterprising mechanics were growing tomatoes on the side. Often, I've found, the reverse of the Friendly City's urban tapestry yields a maze of country threads, as if the woods and farms, imperfectly covered with asphalt, are always waiting for a chance to reclaim their territory.

"I would have liked best to explore all the courtyards," Kracauer wrote, "and search through one room after another." I recognize this feeling. There is a lack of fulfillment in my walks that makes them endlessly tantalizing. I circle the streets and alleys, cross the creek over and over, but what I really want is to enter all the doors, to inhabit every building, to live in that white octagonal house with the curious little balcony, that red cottage dwarfed by the twin pear trees. I want to be on the other side of the windows, looking out at myself on the street. On these marvelous bright days, with clear light falling through my eyelashes, I am so intoxicated by the streets I want to scale the walls, try my teeth on a fence, taste the cobwebs, eat the grass.

What have I forgotten—what am I searching for on these rambles? Some ever-changing, always unforeseen prize: a glint of colored glass or the ruddiness of unexpected tomato plants that throws a new light on the city, altering the whole landscape for a moment, like the pure bands of the rainbow that arced over my in-laws' apartment the other day, transforming the back of the row, with its plain windows and wooden staircases, into a place I'd never seen before.

Desire Paths

T̲h̲e̲y̲ ̲a̲r̲e̲ ̲w̲a̲l̲k̲i̲n̲g̲ up the path that leads from the busy road to the trees. Their sneakers bounce on the tarmac that looks almost violet against the smooth green grass. Car keys jostle in their pockets. Their backpacks shift with the rhythm of their steps. They are heading to class at the big university beyond the pines.

They are crossing the highway on the overpass, staying close to the railing. Cars rush past. On the far side, the railing that has been their safeguard becomes an enemy, as they have to climb over it, balanced on one foot on the small strip of gravel beside the road, in order to reach the shopping plaza. For a moment they teeter there, struggling, the parents just home from work, the kids who seem too small to get over the railing, in danger for a terrifying instant of falling into the oncoming traffic. Then they are on the other side. They go down the steep dirt path, among the weeds, walking sideways, arms out to keep themselves steady, while spotted lanternflies plummet down on them from the tall pole of the streetlight. The path dips to its lowest point, then slopes sharply upward. They climb, passing the smashed watermelon some other shopper has dropped, its red flesh riddled with ants. They reach the parking lot, brush down their clothes to knock off any lingering bugs, and continue toward the doors of the giant store.

We are in the realm of desire paths, on Reservoir Street at the plaza dominated by the Walmart Supercenter.

Desire paths are informal trails worn down by the passage of people or animals. They mark the most efficient routes between locations. They are unplanned but persistent—as vegetation is rubbed away and the paths become clearer, more walkers use them, and the increasing foot traffic deepens the groove in the landscape.

Here on Reservoir Street, observing the two sides of this bustling four-lane road between the shopping plaza and the university, we can see the two responses planners generally take to desire paths. Sometimes the responsible authorities listen to desire. They pave the paths that spring up from the texture of daily life, recognizing them as an expression of the wisdom of the crowd. This is what has happened between the shopping plaza and the university, where students carved a line down the hill to the crosswalk, repeatedly tramping toward the cheap goods at Walmart and the big lot where they park their cars to avoid the high campus fees. Their track was paved, made safe and easy to walk. But on the other side, the one that gives onto a community of townhomes and apartments, we can see the alternate response. Here, desire is ignored. The sidewalk across the overpass comes to an abrupt end. A railing blocks the way.

In Finland, I read, city planners wait for the snow to fall before they create public paths. They follow the footprints of desire. In London, there is an architect who consults dropped cigarette butts and discarded gum to determine where to place a bench.

There's something beautiful about this harmony between designers and the public, between abstract blueprints and lived experience.

Of course, the people in the community that borders Reservoir Street could take an alternate path to the shopping plaza. To be safe, they should walk down to the light at Martin Luther King Jr. Way, cross Market Street on the crosswalk, cross back over Reservoir Street, cross back over Market Street, walk up the hill on the sidewalk, use the crosswalk at Eastover Drive, and then continue over the overpass, eventually meeting up with the students' desire path at the traffic light. This adds about twenty minutes to the walk. Instead of reaching the plaza in ten minutes, they will get there in half an hour. Instead of twenty minutes to go to the store and back, they will have to set aside one hour. For half that time, they will have to carry their laden shopping bags.

Having been, for some years, a full-time working mom, I can attest to the immense difference between twenty minutes and an hour.

But the desire path doesn't listen to me or you. It heeds a need. It responds to hunger. It is not exactly against authority; authority doesn't figure in its calculations. It is not interested in the plan. The signs, the arrows, the helpful warnings placed in its environment, the regular stripes of the zebra crossing, the sidewalk, the traffic light—these signals surround the path without addressing it, like a kind of ambient noise. It will only understand them when they align with its goals, which spring from the logic of here and now, of this apartment and its precise spatial relationship with that grocery aisle, of these minutes leaking away from the clock, these clamoring kids, this shopping list, this fridge that is missing four essential ingredients, this tiredness, this heat or rain, and these muscles that can definitely, certainly, walk a few more steps.

To all of this the desire path listens closely. It leaps up from the cityscape. It flickers over obstacles like lightning. It is so vigorous, so eager, so almost joyful in its progress, it seems as if it might zip right through the shopping plaza, as if it's bent on some clandestine and visionary errand, heading straight for the mountains, or into another life.

October

The Shadowy Street

THE OTHER DAY I was walking along College Avenue, a neighborhood I know well in all its seasons, when a perfectly unfamiliar house suddenly loomed up across the street.

A two-story brick house with white trim, shadowed by an oak. A simple, sturdy structure, built in the foursquare American Craftsman style so popular in the Friendly City, with the requisite porch and tin roof. Is this why I'd never noticed it? Damp-looking concrete steps tinted with lichen. A round table on the porch. A chair with flowered cushions.

I paused and stared, arrested by a mild shock, as if my perception had stumbled.

I've noted two ways to discover newness in a well-known place: You can observe how it changes over time or seek out unexplored paths. But there's a third form of newness, much weirder, perhaps impossible to fully control. Familiarity itself can trick you. Ambling carelessly down a street where you think you know every crack in the sidewalk, you can be ambushed by the sight of a strange door, an alien building, even an entire alley that's never caught your attention before.

This feeling doesn't occur when you visit a place. You have to live there. On a visit, everything is too new to provide the required contrast. It takes repeated exposure to build up a layer of habit, a fabric that can be rent.

There's a wonderful story by the Belgian writer Jean Ray called "The Shadowy Street," first published in 1931. In this chilling tale, a schoolteacher discovers a street called Saint Beregonne's Lane, which no one else can see. It takes the teacher a few seconds to cross the entrance to this lane, which opens between a distillery and a seed merchant's shop, but other people step instantly between the two businesses, insisting they are separated only by a wall. The teacher is startled by this mystery, for he can clearly see the poorly whitewashed walls of the street, its worn, greenish pavement, the sickly viburnum bush sprouting between two doors, and the sign reading Saint Beregonne's Lane. "I concluded that, for everyone in the world except myself, that street existed outside of time and space."

I think of Saint Beregonne's Lane when a house of almond pallor suddenly springs up fully formed on Stuart Street, where I have walked countless times without observing its two front windows, one divided vertically and the other horizontally, or the door painted dark umber, or the two pickup trucks in the driveway. I'm confident that this house doesn't really belong to the secret world of Jean Ray, which turns out to be inhabited by invisible monsters, but the sight of it gives me an eerie yet pleasurable feeling reminiscent of his tale of impossible geography. *It's the shadowy street!* I think when, on one of my night walks, Water Street buckles freakishly to accommodate a long, yellowish building, gloomy and institutional like an office block in a 1970s TV show, whose presence seems to me totally unaccountable. Where did it come from? What is it for? How can such a large structure have materialized out of nowhere? The shadowy street is pressing against the everyday world, cracking its surface, exposing the red and blue neon stripes of the vape shop and the vacant interior of the music equipment store, its filing cabinets illuminated by a night lamp.

A life spent constantly traveling to new places would be deprived of this cunning species of surprise. It's a sensation that always thrills me, because it demonstrates how my brain works, offering a window into my consciousness. How many things the deft, efficient brain skips over in the course of the day! Street scenes erased by a preoccupied glance. Scraps of conversation, overheard and immediately deleted. Words read and forgotten in the pursuit of knowledge.

How could I have missed this extravagantly dilapidated shed collapsing into a pile of chipped red planks? And the palatial structure rising up from Wolfe Street in the twilight, its windowed galleries etched on the misty sky, elegant as the ghost of some Victorian hotel—is that really the bottle factory?

The world is brimming with stuff I don't need. I am enfolded by an unfathomable reservoir of neglected impressions. To glimpse the shadowy street is to peer for a moment into those depths, which, for the practical purposes of my daily life, might as well exist outside of time and space. Maybe Jean Ray was right to represent its darkness as terror, for what would life be like if you noticed every single thing? That level of attention might well be intolerable. But in small doses, these flashes of awareness produce a double wonder: astonishment at my own capacity to ignore my surroundings, and amazement at the richness of the world.

An Attempt at Exhausting Court Square

USUALLY, I WALK around the city; this week, I decided to let the city walk around me.

A few weeks ago, I picked up a little volume called *An Attempt at Exhausting a Place in Paris,* by the experimental writer Georges Perec (famous for having written a novel without using the letter *e*). In October 1974, Perec spent three days in the Place Saint-Sulpice, writing down everything he observed. He wasn't interested in the landmarks—the district council building, the church, the cafés—but what he called "the rest": "that which is generally not taken note of, that which is not noticed, that which has no importance: what happens when nothing happens other than the weather, people, cars, and clouds."

Here's an example of Perec's writing in the book:
It is 6:45 p.m.
Autos go by
A yellow postal van stops in front of the mailbox, which a postal worker relieves of its dual contents (Paris/Out of Town, including suburbs)
It's still raining
I'm drinking a Salers Gentian.
I was intrigued by this project. Is it possible to exhaust a

place? I didn't have a whole weekend to spend on the experiment, but I thought I could manage one day. I decided to sit at the café across from the courthouse during opening hours, from seven in the morning until six in the evening, and attempt to exhaust this place.

...

7:05 a.m. Four men in baseball caps and sneakers come into the café, then a man alone with his laptop. A school bus passes.

The lights are on in the beautiful courthouse. Seated at a table outside, close to the sidewalk, I can see into the offices. Picture frames hang crowded together on the walls. Halloween mobiles dangle paper spiders and pumpkins. Out front, a banner with a picture of a sugar skull announces the Skeleton Festival.

A man with a businesslike air, wearing a checkered shirt and flowered bowtie, enters the café.

Across the street, on the steps of the district court, a woman with a smooth white bob smokes contemplatively, resting her arm on the wall, watching the brightening sky.

A pink edge of cloud shows beyond the high stone balcony of the courthouse. Does anyone ever stand up there?

The square is quiet, as if half asleep. Subdued stained glass of the Presbyterian church: a marine palette of green, lavender, and gray.

The businesslike man in the bowtie leaves the café. A drowsy-looking woman follows, eating banana bread from a box.

An officer in a brown uniform crosses the street, carrying a heavy-looking black bag, and enters the door of the courthouse marked Exit Only.

The man in the bowtie returns, looking at his watch. He must have been strolling around the courthouse. He tries the door of the district court, but it's locked. He waits on the step, reading the signs on the wall.

A balding, vaping man in shades goes by, wearing bright blue sweatpants, accompanied by a tiny dog.

A woman carrying two bags goes up the steps of the district court, passing the man in the bowtie, and a guard lets her in. Bowtie, looking a bit crestfallen, walks down the steps to wait on the sidewalk.

The bell on the courthouse clock tower tolls eight o'clock.

The square is waking up. A beeping truck stops outside the restaurant next door, its hazard lights blinking. In front it says Thermo King; on the side, Schenk Foods – Since 1928.

Bowtie has finally entered the court!

A silver-haired man in a black shirt stands on the sidewalk near my table, looking around, waiting for someone.

The driver of the truck enters the café, pushing a dolly loaded with crates of milk.

The silver man's friend arrives: a man with salt-and-pepper hair in a sage-green polo shirt. "Good to see you!" "It's been a while!" "It has!" "You've been around the world!"

A man in a cap and work boots, a camouflage-pattern

phone case at his belt, sets up a sign on the corner: Road Work Ahead.

Three prisoners cross from the district court building to the courthouse, cuffed together, escorted by officers. Two wear orange jumpsuits; one is in red and white stripes. They shuffle along in their ill-fitting slippers and ankle chains, taking the steps one at a time, and go through the Exit Only door.

People go in and out of the café. Young people who look like students arrive with wet hair. A bald man leaves his lovely chocolate-brown dog tied to the railing while he buys his coffee; it gazes after him with whiskey-colored eyes.

Bowtie is back. He wanders past the café, looking around in a concerned way, almost turning in circles, as if watching for someone who might appear from any direction.

A parking attendant in a green vest, sunglasses strapped around his bald head, lumbers down the sidewalk, checking the cars.

A man with a backpack sits on the steps of the district court, apparently waiting for someone, vaping and drinking from a can.

There are many backpacks in the city. Also a lot of baldness.

The sun slips past the courthouse, lighting the street, the lawn, and the edge of the pale stone church.

A young woman stands in the light on the corner, fluffing up her hair and taking selfies. When she gets into her car, another car stops beside her; the driver wants her parking space, but she tells him no, sorry, she's not leaving, and directs him down the street.

She sits in her car, which is badly dented on one side, and puts on her glasses.

What is the happiness of writing all this down?

Leafy trees. A young woman with a massive neuroscience textbook. A whitish-blue sky, the horizon almost too bright to look at.

Inmates in jumpsuits, more officers with heavy bags (could it be their lunch?), four people with camera equipment talking on the courthouse lawn. Bowtie lingers nearby, looking at some papers, checking his phone. He sits down on the courthouse steps.

A man in a brown suit, light-blue shirt, and pink tie, with a leather satchel over his shoulder, walks slowly from his car to the district court. He goes up the steps gingerly, gripping the railing. Contrast his arduous progress with the energy of the selfie-taking woman, who springs from her car, smiles at the photographers on the lawn, and asks their permission to pass. They wave her on politely.

One thing about the relationship between life and writing: Life has more. It takes very little life to fill up a page of a notebook.

Bowtie reappears, talking animatedly to a woman dressed all in black. They walk toward the courthouse together.

A woman in flip-flops with neatly curled bangs leaves the

district court, carrying some papers. She squints at the sun through her glasses and drives away in her old maroon car.

A man with twins in a double stroller enters the café. A woman in clacking high heels, wearing a surgical mask. A woman in orange clogs, discreet little tattooed flowers showing on her wrist against the cuff of her trench coat.

This square, where almost nothing is happening, is so interesting I can't look away! The woman all in black, who walked off with Bowtie, has reappeared on the corner, talking into her phone, which she holds some distance from her face. Bowtie paces in the background.

A man leaves the district court at a run, dashes to his parked car, flings his backpack inside it, and runs back into the court.

Selfie reappears, wearing her glasses and carrying a bag. Taking long strides in her striped pants, she enters the district court.

On the corner, All Black texts, then makes another call, while Bowtie waits. Somebody is missing from their party. All Black gestures emphatically as she speaks—pointing, waving, circling her hand—but she's smiling, as if she can see the humor in the situation.

The sun has reached me. Cobwebs glisten where the railing of the café meets the wall. I blow a small insect from my hand.

The café is full. A lively atmosphere. For some time, I have not heard the courthouse bells. Fragments of conversation on the breeze. "There's so much beauty there, even when it's raining." "He doesn't *have* characteristics. He *is* characteristics."

I look up from writing, and Bowtie and All Black have disappeared. Good luck to them!

Perec: *Obvious limits to such an undertaking: even when my goal is just to observe, I don't see what takes place a few meters from me: I don't notice, for example, that cars are parking.*

. . .

Obvious limits to such an undertaking. Now, compiling my notes, I realize I've written a small book, maybe as long as the one Perec wrote in three days, certainly too long to include it all here. They go on for pages, the people of the square, the men in neon vests examining the road with an orange level, the woman in the pearl necklace who hangs her jacket neatly in the back of her car, the biker with turquoise-streaked hair, the slouching man reading a book at one of the café tables without ordering anything, the child in the purple dress dotted with white hearts, the woman with dyed red hair carrying a life-size ceramic duck. Selfie runs wildly across the road, drops her phone, retrieves it, dives into her car, and emerges wearing a different jacket. Clouds cover the sun. So many people I know appear—coworkers, students, a woman I met once while waiting for a train. I see Bowtie and All Black again, standing on the courthouse lawn with another woman and a child who bounces around while the adults talk, windmilling his arms and improvising karate moves, the long sleeves of his hoodie flapping. But I'll have to leave them out—all the children, the dogs, the changing sky, the different notebooks and binders, the tattoos, the phones, the keys. I will not be able to exhaust, in writing, even half a day in this place, or begin to describe the feeling that autumn is near.

The Voice of the City

THE CITY SPEAKS through its signs. We Went Solar; So Can You. Mutt-urity Matters: Adopt or Foster an Adult Dog. Walking in the city, circling through the neighborhoods in the lemony, early-autumn light, my eyes are open to the city's voice, its remarks on the season: Give Thanks, Happy Fall Y'all, Happy Halloween. Gourds and pumpkins on porches add their golden commentary. Cardboard gravestones murmur R. I. P. and Trick or Treat. And in this election season, under the shade of the stirring, still-green leaves, Trump-Vance, Harris-Walz, Ben Cline, Kaine 2024, an anachronistic Trump 2020 sign, Biden-Harris with the *Biden* covered with duct tape, Javier for City Council, Re-Elect Deanna Reed. Lists of candidates for the school board with check marks beside their names. A chorus of voices, dissonant among pots of brightly colored mums, in the weeds, propped against the garages, opinions and wishes and confessions, A Spoiled-Rotten Dog Lives Here, Black Lives Matter, Butterfly Crossing, Open for Prayer, Free Palestine, Hate Has No Home Here, Slow Your Roll, Home Sweet Home. There's the board with three stripes of bold color proclaiming, in three different languages, "No matter where you are from, we're glad you're our neighbor," a sign created right here in the Friendly City, which has now spread all over the country, and which we used to have in our own yard until it was torn down and ripped to pieces by persons unknown—one of a very few truly unfriendly incidents we've experienced here.

Our unfriendliest encounter was provoked by a sign. We had been to a small rally at the courthouse, and were walking home with some family friends, with our kids and their kids, who were in elementary and middle school at the time. My husband carried a homemade sign on his shoulder. As we passed a downtown restaurant, one of the diners, seeing us through the window, became so enraged at the sight of our sign that he got up from his table and ran out the door to swear at us from across the street. We glanced at him and kept walking. The kids jumped up and down, beside themselves with excitement. "Did he say the f-word?" I remember being amazed at the passion of this man, strong enough to interrupt his dinner and send him hurtling out of the restaurant, undeterred by the presence of children. But he had heard the voice of our sign, and he answered it in his own way. His voice and ours, inextricably entangled, are tones in a larger wave of sound, the voice of the city itself—a motley pattern represented by the new mural on the public school building downtown, embodied in the multicolored leaves of the design created by local students and given the hopeful or maybe just descriptive title *Intertwined*.

The city doesn't need words to speak. It speaks in color, in painted buildings, in flags on porches rippling out their rainbows, their stars and stripes. And doesn't it speak in the yards themselves—not just their signs but their flowers, their mown or unmown grass, their neat borders or piles of debris? And what about the cars? I don't speak car myself—I have only the foggiest understanding of the dialect—but to someone this ancient Mustang parked on the corner must mean something, and this truck, and this hybrid plugged into the wall. The shiny cars, the grimy cars, the cars that limp through the streets bearing the wounds of honorable or dishonorable combat, the ramshackle car in a yard with a neighbor's legs poking out from under it—all have a voice for those who can hear. And the cars speak, as well, with their vanity plates, so common you can tell this is a Virginia town, our personalized plates being the cheapest in the country, so that a single afternoon's walk absorbs a cacophony of notes, jaunty, funny, religious, arcane: DUKE GAL, KLUMPY, KAFN8ED, PRVRB 31, LUC1FUR, GAKRAK, MRHOOD, DROP. And then there are the bumper stickers—"Shop Local," "Save the Bay," "My boss is a Jewish carpenter," "My kid beat up your honor student," "Senior driver—please be patient," "Some days you just have to create your own sunshine," and the venerable "I ♥ Dog Food Smell." Many of these stickers are found in towns around the country, but each place, I reflect, watching the cars from the bridge on Martin Luther King Jr. Way, must have its own particular mixture of these ingredients, its unique anthology of bumper philosophy. The cars, whizzing past me, go on talking, adding their words to the voice of the city, succinctly—"God Guns Trump"—or at greater length: "'In a time of deceit, telling the truth is a revolutionary act'—George Orwell."

I once read that style is the outer manifestation of a method. Style is a way of doing. It's the way you do your hair, your shopping, your chores. Leaving the bridge as evening falls, walking home on the west side of 42, I realize that the voice of the city also includes the personal style of its citizens, that elaborate visual language. All the hats, the tattoos, the yards of flannel. The comfortable shoes. The buzzcuts and dreadlocks. The young girls crossing the street in front of me, their hair pinned and glistening, wearing stiff flounced dresses, perhaps on their way to a quinceañera. The goth kid skipping up a driveway with a glee that contrasts starkly with a melancholy T-shirt reading "Love is a smoke made with the fume of sighs." What would it take to hear the city's voice in all its myriad reverberations? Outside a small house, some Mennonites in plain clothing stand gazing up at the sky, the women's heads tilted back in little white caps, and I discover for the first time that plain people live here, something that immediately makes sense, considering their impeccably tidy yard. They glance at me, smile, wave, and go back to watching the sky, on the lookout for some celestial phenomenon I'm not aware of, or waiting for the moon to emerge from the clouds, or reading the book of the stars—a text that strikes me, tonight, as only slightly more complex than the voice of the city.

Ordinary Miracles

BRIGHT FALL. On College Street, a tree glows as yellow as the Dead End sign. Spear-shaped leaves flutter down, making diagonal chains of gold.

Leaves fly on the wind, crunch underfoot in an earth-toned mass, pile up in tumbled flames along the sidewalk.

This street runs into a forest, which shimmers at the end of the block. The trees are still green, but just turning, so that the air is green and gold, the sunlight shining through the leaves with their varying jewellike colors: emerald, amber, a few deep ruby notes.

Color belongs to change, not eternity, says Lucretius. In the realm of color, nothing is fixed. Depending on the light, a dove's throat may appear red or blue. As things decay and disintegrate with the passage of time, they lose their color, like purple wool pulled apart into smaller and smaller threads, scattering its substance until it breathes away all its brilliance.

Time is what I'm feeling, time in this redbud tree with its broad, trembling leaves, their green touched with bronze. Time in the maple already stripped of half its wealth, so that its branches appear to be strung with little red lights, while a rustling carpet spreads about it on the ground, rosy as a field of chopped pink lady apples. How marvelous that the passage of time can cause a change in color that feels like a gain rather than a loss. The first trees to turn announce their presence along with their imminent decline, holding up torches that blaze out from the green background, vibrating against the flat blue sky.

In *Pilgrim at Tinker Creek*, which Annie Dillard wrote in the woods about a hundred miles from here, she describes "the tree with the lights in it." Dillard writes of a girl, born blind, who became sighted after surgery, and was led into a garden. The girl, amazed, held on to a tree she perceived as full of light. For a long time after reading this, Dillard confesses, she searched for that tree. "Then one day I was walking along Tinker Creek thinking of nothing at all and I saw the tree with the lights in it. I saw the backyard cedar where the mourning doves roost charged and transfigured, each cell buzzing with flame."

Dillard's tree didn't really have lights in it, any more than the tree in the garden where a newly sighted girl clung to a branch. These are effects of perception. They are awakenings: sudden visions that arise from the concord of objects, angles of light, the time of day. They are the outcome of chance, which makes autumn feel like a lucky season. It's not only the ripeness, the bounty of gardens and fields, that gives an air of good fortune to this time of year; it's also the flood of opportunities, offered with each changing leaf, to perceive things differently, to see the tree with the lights in it.

It's so bright out this afternoon, so brisk, both warm and cold, incredibly clear, there's no one outside, a dog barks in one of the houses as I pass, there are pumpkins and scarecrows on the porches, fake cobwebs in the bushes, a longhaired cat stretched sleepily in a driveway, a row of potted plants, a baby swing, a pile of laundry baskets, a dusty van, a clutch of lawn furniture heaped up higgledy-piggledy, wind chimes tinkling away, kids' bicycles and toys in the grass, and this, right now, is the town with the lights in it. A leaf on the curb, chocolate at the base, saffron at the tip. A big flossy pine leaning over the street, dangling its cones, looking like a queenly grandmother coming into the room, her sleeves hanging down covered with baubles, with more cones clustered at the top like a heavy, slightly tacky but magnificent studded necklace. A hot-pink burning bush. Dogwood leaves in matte red, translucent where the sun strikes them. Colors so intense they look synthetic. Above the houses, as I turn around at the dead end, a puffy, red-gold tree that seems inflated, blown up against the sky, spun up there like a plume of cotton candy in a festive, sticky-sweet, orange creamsicle flavor.

In autumn, time itself becomes revelatory. The most basic and ordinary thing—the turning of the earth—presses color out of the landscape, making the trees flare up, setting smokeless fires along the ridge. I climb the hill, panting a bit in the sun, and the city spreads out below me, a haze of green flecked with bubbles of ochre, chestnut, and red. The peak of Massanutten rises above it, a glorious shade of mauve, the purple mountain majesty of the old song. And to my surprise, in this deserted spot, a woman comes striding toward me, bearing two onions in her outstretched hand. Like a personification of the season, she passes me with a sprightly step, her face gilded with light and an expression of unrestrained joy.

I stare after her. Can such an extreme state of happiness really be achieved through a pair of onions? One would think they were the last onions in the valley, an essential ingredient in a meal of unsurpassable significance and splendor, without which the life of this woman, and no doubt a great many precious friends and relations—or, who knows, perhaps the entire city, the nation, the planet—would be damaged beyond hope of repair. And she managed to find them! Yanked them from a field at the last second! Triumph, elation! Only a drama of this kind, I feel, can account for her private and radiant bliss—that, or the season, wafting her jubilant frame up Summit Avenue, tossing her white hair on the wind like snow.

The Ghost of Evelyn Byrd

FOR HALLOWEEN, I thought I'd try to walk in the footsteps of a neighborhood phantom. But the local ghosts proved hard to find. While inexplicable lights and creaks have been reported in certain old houses, and there have even been ghost tours of the city, the documentation on the subject is vague and thin. Marguerite duPont Lee's *Virginia Ghosts*—a book full of intrigue, offering anecdotes like "The Haunted Kitchen" and "Telekinesis in Lynchburg"—doesn't mention the Friendly City or even the surrounding county. The two-volume set of *The Ghosts of Virginia* by L. B. Taylor Jr. contains some fascinating lore, such as "The Spectral Canine of Goochland," "Aunt Esther's Ghostly Pumpkin Pie," "Chased by a Dead Horse," and my personal favorite, "The Ghosts Who Love to Read"—but the Friendly City receives hardly any notice, the nearest apparition materializing in Bridgewater.

I did come across a ghost named Evelyn Byrd, however, which immediately recalled our own Evelyn Byrd Avenue. Could there be a connection? Legend tells that Evelyn Byrd, born in 1707, was forbidden to marry the man she loved (perhaps because he was a Catholic). She died at the age of thirty, allegedly of a broken heart. Since then, she has made a number of appearances around her family's old plantation in

Charles City County, often dressed in white. A gentle specter, she is reported to drift about in a quiet way without scaring anybody, which makes her seem like the right type of ghost to be honored in the Friendly City, but why would we choose a phantom from so far away?

One of the nice things about living in a smallish town is that it's easy to get your city surveyor on the phone. I called ours, and found him eager to help. No, he said, he doubted the street was named after the ghostly Evelyn Byrd. He suggested a more recent person of that name, who had lived here in the city: Evelyn Byrd Deyerle, born in 1906, the sister of Dr. Henry Deyerle, who had been a prominent figure when roads were being built on that side of town. Since there is a Deyerle Avenue running parallel to Evelyn Byrd, it seemed I had my answer. A trip to the public library, where an obliging librarian helped me search through the genealogy shelves, confirmed the identity and local residence of Evelyn Byrd Deyerle. So *our* Evelyn Byrd was born two hundred years after the one in the ghost story. But did that mean there was no link between them?

I dug into the genealogies and found... *so many Evelyn Byrds*. Evelyn Byrd Nelson Page. Evelyn Byrd Page Lee. Evelyn Byrd Beverly Lee. Evelyn Byrd Page Wood. The name proliferated, rising through history like an unquiet spirit. I started to feel like I was trapped in an echo chamber, or perhaps a labyrinth in a spooky movie, spinning around while a voice from some invisible source whispered variations of the same name in my ear.

I come from a family with some repetitive naming traditions. Certain names in my father's family are so common, people who hold them have to be identified by place or other details (as a child, it seemed perfectly normal to me to have an uncle called Ahmed Milwaukee). In my husband's Amish family tree, as if the recurrent Millers and Yoders weren't enough, there are generations of women named Barbara. So I'm used to the idea of reusing names. But as I scrolled through dizzying records, tracking the Evelyn Byrds sprinkled among the Harrisons, Bollings, and Taylors, it seemed to me that the somewhat presumptuously designated First Families of Virginia had a clannish intensity of name repetition even the Amish couldn't beat. The name Evelyn Byrd—conveniently gender-neutral for many years—goes back at least to the ghostly Evelyn's father, William Evelyn Byrd. It extends to the distinguished archaeologist Evelyn Byrd Harrison and the aviator Richard Evelyn Byrd. There is even a quite awful novel called *Evelyn Byrd*. Recently, according to her Instagram, the actor Byrdie Bell—nickname of Evelyn Byrd Bell—visited the home of her phantasmal ancestress, whom she calls "the first Evelyn Byrd."

And what's it like to walk on Evelyn Byrd Avenue? Well, it's pretty dreary. There's a dullness here on even the most brilliant fall afternoon, a sense of emptiness to the road between the chain stores and chain restaurants that leads you up the hill to the chain hotels. This is a place to drive through, where a steady flood of cars flows between the state university and the highway. It's a road that discourages lingering, wearying the eye with a string of almost identical structures, standardized signs and storefronts, clipped bushes in a row. At University Boulevard, the sidewalk peters out, leaving a would-be walker stranded amid the traffic. I think I'll turn around here, because if I keep walking, I know I'm only going to see more of the same.

There's something inherently ghostly about repetition. A ghost is sometimes called a revenant—one who returns. Maybe there's a certain logic to the conjunction of a well-worn family name and a road lined with parking lots and retail chains. Still, I sense a difference in energy between these two styles of repetition. The name Evelyn Byrd surely carries its own historical hauntings, but it also belonged to a person who lived here, unlike Beach Bum Tanning, Texas Roadhouse, or AT&T.

Feeling a little morose after my walk, I curl up with *The Ghosts of Virginia* to reread "The Happy Grave of Adam Kersh." This report concerns a deceased cabinetmaker, familiarly known as Uncle Ad, who appears on starry nights to sit on his tombstone near Bridgewater and while away the hours playing his fiddle. I'd gladly adopt, for the Friendly City, this amiable and sensitive ghost, who is said to select his music according to his listener's mood: "A toe-tapping melody, a bright tune for those who have a happy heart; a sad dirge for those of dour disposition."

November

Murmuration

ON THAT DAY, when you weren't sure where to go, you remembered the words of a neighbor. "Take a walk on Hawkins Street," he suggested. "It's best when the school buses are letting out. It really shows what's special about the city."

So you walked toward Hawkins Street through the hot, bright air, among the skeletal trees, the dry leaves stirring and crackling underfoot. How quickly they seemed to have fallen. A few branches still held up the shreds of their gorgeous colors, smoldering lonely among the rooftops. In Liberty Park, the gingko trees, which had turned later than the others, raised their golden pyramids. A prison crew was working in the park, dressed in zebra-striped pants and orange T-shirts, the drone of their leaf blowers erasing the sound of the traffic. The sky was an opaline blue, streaked with white. It seemed to have grown larger as the trees dropped their foliage, revealing more of its pallor through the bare branches, and this, along with the dryness of the air, the tea-like fragrance of fallen leaves, and the subtle change in the angle of the light, convinced you that it really was autumn, despite the heat, which you persisted in describing as unseasonable. How long, you wondered, would you go on saying this, as if warm weather this late in the year was something extraordinary? You remembered the children who had recently come trick-ortreating at your door, pouring with sweat in their furry costumes.

In Old Town, political signboards stood in the yards, rattling in the feverish wind. Some had fallen over in the grass. You walked up Bruce Street past the cemetery, thinking that soon, once the temperature dropped, it would be the time of murmuration. You'd heard that it was possible, in the autumn and winter months, to see the murmuration of starlings in the city: the birds flocking together at dawn and dusk, making entrancing patterns in the sky to the rhythmic murmur of wings. You'd only seen it in videos online, and hoped to catch it live one day. In a book about bird behavior, you'd read that starlings sleep communally, and that there are several theories about why they form murmurations above their roosting sites, "flying," the scientist wrote, "in great weaving clouds." They might be warding off predators by banding together to make big, dramatic motions. They might be conserving the heat of the flock. They might be broadcasting information about feeding sites. Or they might be indulging in a form of avian play.

You arrived at Hawkins Street, a small branch off Reservoir Street that slopes down toward a blue wall of mountains, thinking of murmuration, of how things gather in response to pressure, thousands of starlings, long lines of people at polling places, leaves blown out of the street to form rustling banks along the curb, piled together in jostling layers, driven by force.

Who will read the patterns of these things?

On Hawkins Street, there were small houses and a few midsized apartment buildings. You passed a tiny porch decorated with rows of hanging plants, then a slender yard packed with living and artificial flowers. A rocking chair. A complicated fountain festooned with mosses and animal statues. A strip of earth where a plaster Virgin Mary, her blue sleeves outspread, shared space with a chipped black laughing buddha and a second, calmer buddha head, its face painted white with crimson lips. A man talking on a cell phone waved at you from between a pair of parked trucks. A woman holding a baby waved at you from a doorway. A teenager in a wheelchair, shepherded by three women, made his way across the street to a car, where the women helped him in, and all of them waved at you. And when the school bus arrived, you understood why your friend had recommended this neighborhood, why he had found it so illustrative of the essence of the city, for this was a place where the Friendly City expressed its character as a nesting town. Kids clambered down from the bus, chatting in the city's second tongue. Yard signs proclaimed both Slower Is Safer and Más Lento, Más Seguro. At the crosswalk on Reservoir Street, where some teens were waiting to cross with younger children, an automated voice announced in two languages that the yellow pedestrian lights were flashing (the cars, ignorant of all human speech, kept surging by). A sign posted at a construction site bore the name of an electrical company called Neza and a logo of a stylized coyote with an ornate collar: the emblem of Nezahualcoyotl, the renowned Aztec poet-king, who died in 1472.

Though his name is translated as Hungry Coyote or Fasting Coyote, Nezahualcoyotl often identified himself with a bird in his poems. "Nezahualcoyotl has become a bird," he declared. "I, a quetzal feather, a bird of the flowering water, I flow in celebration. I am a song."

Walking home, you thought of the flowing birds, the patterns of movement all over the earth, the pressing desires for warmth, for play, for communal sleep. The leaves blown willy-nilly against the walls. You remembered arriving in this city, which you hoped never to leave, and you also thought of your father, who left his country to nest elsewhere, something that was unusual at the time, and how ordinary it became later, during the war, the ongoing violence, a force still pushing desperate people all over the globe. You remembered how your father and uncles talked about the war, their horror and astonishment, their helpless gestures as they spoke of this overwhelming catastrophe that seemed, and still seems, to have no end, and which they could never have imagined when they were young, when they walked together in a lovely, unspoiled city by the sea—a city they still remember for its white walls, its courteous, slow-paced life, its happiness, its innocence, and its friendliness.

Small Fates

Wandering through Woodbine Cemetery, I thought I might write some small fates.

In 1906, the French writer Félix Fénéon created a new form of literature, writing pithy little stories of just a few lines for a Paris newspaper. This sort of thing had been common in the papers since the nineteenth century; the short announcements, based on news items, were used to fill in blank spots in the layout, and were known as *fait-divers*, usually translated as "small fates." But Fénéon revolutionized the practice, using his irony and wit to transform this space filler into a literary genre. A collection of his small fates was published under the title *Nouvelles en trois lignes*, which can mean either "the news in three lines" or "novellas in three lines."

Fénéon's small fates often contain a wry comment or twist: "Strikers in Ronchamp, Haute-Saône, threw in the river a worker who insisted on continuing his labor." With a deadpan tone, they point out things that are surprising or absurd: "In Le Brabant, Vosges, M. Amet-Chevrier, 42, and his wife, 39, are from now on the parents of 19 children." Since newspapers report on crime and violence, the terseness of the small fates can give their humor a caustic edge: "Scheid, of Dunkirk, fired three times at his wife. Since he missed every shot, he decided to aim at his mother-in-law, and connected."

A small fate is concise, like the writing on a tombstone, which indicates a whole life with a name and a pair of numbers. From the dates, you can tell whether a person died old or young. You can guess at historical events that might have had an influence: an outbreak of disease or a war. From the nearby stones, you can sometimes connect the members of a family. But that's all. Those who bore these names were here, they lived, and they died, and all those years—all the experiences, loves and hatreds, frustrations and hopes—are summed up briefly in a carven sign.

Catbirds squalled in the high trees. The weather was finally beginning to turn, and I walked with my hands in the pockets of my jacket. The mountains in the distance made a collage: a dark line of forest pasted onto the solid blue of the ridge, and behind them the canvas of the sky, pale where it met the mountains. I never find it depressing or morbid to saunter in a cemetery. The old graves, obelisks, and family mausoleums can have a calming effect, encouraging one to take the long view. The mute stones are a reminder that the stresses of life, its strife and uproar, and even its most horrible events will end in silence.

Fénéon's small fates adopt a similar perspective. In these laconic lines, everyone's story shrinks to a scrap of newspaper filler. As I walked, I reflected that the small fate might be the right form for a small city, where people live lives of limited influence, and no one is expected to play a major role in the events of the day. Our newspaper reports are of merely local interest. I thought I might make some good small fates out of the crimes described there. I remembered stories I'd heard that could serve as material, like the one about the housebreaker who, surprised in the night, jumped out a window and fled, but was easily identified afterward because he'd left his prosthetic leg on the lawn. Or the one about the would-be burglar who banged on a door, claiming to be a police officer, and whose trick failed because, as the inhabitants of the house could see clearly in the porch light, he had neglected to put on a shirt.

And there was the break-in at our house, too—surely a petty crime, emblematic of the misdeeds of ordinary people in a commonplace town. One night we awoke to a sound of shattering glass. Dulled by sleep, we assumed one of our kids had dropped something in the dark. We saw a cell phone light glinting on the stairs, which we also took as belonging to one of our teenagers. In my groggy state, I found it odd, but not shocking, that this kid was wearing sneakers in the middle of the night, which I could hear squeaking on the floor.

My husband got up to investigate and found the living-room floor covered with glass from a broken pane in our front door. The intruder had simply reached in and unlatched it. (Prospective burglars, please note that we have installed better locks!) He was now sitting on the couch, clad in a hoodie and texting on his phone, for all the world like our own son, but although he was young—in his early twenties, based on my husband's best guess in the dark—he was definitely not our child.

"Sir," my husband said sternly, "you need to leave."

Oh, the ineptitude of small-town crooks. Their pitiful, flaky schemes. They will never get into the history books. Not one of them will destroy a river or start a war halfway around the world. What was this ninny doing? Slumped on the couch, he seemed hardly aware that he was in somebody else's house. I imagine him sending disappointed texts to a friend or accomplice ("They don't even have a TV!"). Ordered to leave, he obediently went outside. My husband suspected he was deeply under the influence of some drug. Lacking the sense to leave the scene of the crime, he sat down on our front steps. My husband had to shoo him off the place.

In the cemetery, I walked up to the pretty little chapel, admiring its greenish, coppery doors and art nouveau rosettes, thinking of our small thief, remembering how we called the police more for his protection than ours—if he'd broken into the house next door, our well-armed neighbor might have shot this addled boy. The chapel was locked, as usual. I peered through the bars at the window on the far wall, whose stained glass filled the interior with color: an image of Jesus in a red robe, cradling a lamb of brilliant whiteness, surrounded by an aquamarine sky. Such vibrancy hidden behind the stone walls, like the life behind a name, or the drama and suffering behind one of Fénéon's small fates. I realized I'd already thought too much about our break-in, and even now I was wondering what had happened to that young man. And I knew I would never write my small fates, because I couldn't get into the right mindset. None of our fates seemed small to me.

The Image of the City

THERE IS A FOREST near my house, but I've never walked there. I can see it from the bike path that branches off from Third Street, where I often ramble, but a fence separates me from the dense trees that beckon across the distance, raising their rusty branches against the sky.

Today I'm taking a new route, hoping to reach the forest from a different direction. I start off toward Market Street from the Baptist church. The hill drops steeply behind the farm equipment store, and I scuttle down crabwise, then tramp through the deep weeds, threading my way between sheds and ranks of tractors. One of the pleasures of walking is getting personal with space, encountering your surroundings at a granular level. The feedback from the ground underfoot, the textures of grass and concrete, and the unexpected conjunctions of objects that meet the eye—crates, slats, ladders, frames, white drums marked Used Oil in red paint, with the green hill behind them, topped with the triangular brick church—all this adds up to a vivid image of a place, charged with sensory detail and deeply satisfying.

In his 1960 book *The Image of the City*, the urban planner Kevin Lynch studied the mental maps people make of the cities where they live. "This book is about the look of cities," he writes in the preface, "and whether this look is of any importance, and whether it can be changed. The urban landscape, among its many roles, is also something to be seen, to be remembered, and to delight in."

Lynch's book, which would have a lasting influence in the field of behavioral geography, explores cities much bigger than ours—Boston, Los Angeles, and Jersey City. But his findings are relevant to any person moving through a space. Each of us, he explains, creates "an environmental image, the generalized mental picture of the exterior physical world." This image is composed of sensations and memory. It's more complex and flexible than a map, and varies from person to person. It helps us interpret information and make decisions, and affects the way we feel about our environment. "The need to recognize and pattern our surroundings is so crucial, and has such long roots in the past, that this image has wide practical and emotional importance to the individual."

Under a pewter-gray, semitransparent sky, I walk up Market Street, a fairly unlovely stretch of road, wondering what Kevin Lynch, with his quest for urban beauty, would make of this For Lease sign with a grinning face outside a mud-colored warehouse. I imagine he wouldn't be very impressed. But I think he'd approve of the way Market Street sweeps along Westover Park, since clear trajectories, gentle slopes, and ample green space are all elements of his ideal city design. I remember, as well, that he cautions against too much organization in the urban environment, which can feel "monotonous or restrictive." A perfectly controlled and tidy city would also be perfectly boring. "It is important to main-tain some great common forms," he writes. "But within this large framework, there should be a certain plasticity, a richness of possible structures and clues," so that each of us can construct an individual image of our urban space.

My own mental map of the city is a scratched and scribbled thing, with plenty of arrows, question marks, crossed-out bits, and corrections. With my poor sense of direction, I am hardly a natural cartographer. It takes me a long time to get to know a place, and I find it disorienting to speed through a landscape in a car. I need to get onto the street, even a dullish street like this one, and feel its contours with the soles of my boots. This method has its advantages. The leisurely pace of a walk allows surprising sights to crystallize from the landscape: a glimpse of mountains framed by the pergola of the bank, or a colorful composition of white chicken feathers blown among red rosebushes. And when you walk, you can extend, adjust, and fill in your private atlas at the speed for which your organism evolved, not snatching quick impressions from the driver's seat but crunching over this gravel behind the bank, passing the office of the quarry, and watching the forest rise into view, its edge snapping into your map, no longer fenced off but close by, within reach, with its piney smell.

I think this forest must belong to the quarry. Gazing into its fringes, I see signs prohibiting hunting and trespassing. Brownish veins in the shadows suggest the lines of a wire fence. But surely it's possible to go a little closer. I watch for a break in the traffic and cross Waterman Drive, where I come up against a trench lined with large, loose stones of the anklespraining variety, almost certainly meant to deter would-be trespassers.

I've met the owners of this quarry. A mutual friend introduced us years ago. Dear neighbors, I'm just taking the briefest peep into your forest! I scramble across the stones and through a gap between the trunks, where there's no fence, and duck inside the rugged grove. The sound of the traffic recedes with startling swiftness, as if I've passed through the portal to another world. Turkey vultures circle among the treetops. I hear the thin, sawlike creak of insects. A leaf falls, crisp as an intake of breath. Peering out through the branches, I see houses I know, the back of a street where I've walked completely cut off from this wood. Only now do I graft the forest onto my environmental image, with its blowsy cedars, leaf-strewn trails, and strands of sylvan light.

Since a mental map is built of memory and sensation, walking maps must be more intricate and layered than driving ones, simply because they take more time. I think of my mother, who takes only short strolls now, supported by her cane, and how attuned she is to changes in her environment, noticing every bump in the sidewalk, observing how grass grows between the cracks, and registering the finest seasonal shifts in the tree by her back door.

Pedestrian Secrets

Steps

ON THANKSGIVING, when I was a child, there was always a terrible moment at the table when we were invited—*commanded* might be a better word—to say what we were thankful for. The ritual was annual; I don't know why I was never prepared. Beneath the eager stares of the adults, who seemed as hungry for my answer as I was for the cranberry sauce, every nice thing in the world flew out of my head. But this time around, I know what to say. This year, my year of walking in the Friendly City, I am thankful for the steps: the secluded pedestrian steps, half concealed by walls and foliage, that offer safe passage to local walkers.

There are three sets of steps along Martin Luther King Jr. Way, connecting the residential neighborhoods with the university. I wonder if they were desire paths once—if students used to scramble up and down the incline, trying to get to class, before the steps were built. Now the stairs are worn, cracked in places, almost like part of the earth. Weeds border them. Ragged trees hang over them. These moldering flights feel clandestine, otherworldly, as if they don't quite belong to everyday life (students apparently think so too: I once startled a pair of them quietly smoking a joint on the steps below Ott

Street). For a walker, there is an air of magic to these steps, which materialize in the undergrowth as if in answer to a wish, as if the genie of the city has bowed to your command and, with an occult gesture, transported you to a different level of the street.

If these convenient passages have the aura of *A Thousand and One Nights*, how much more enchanting are the stairways that lead nowhere! The steps in the wall of the funeral home that plunge straight into a bush—what gnome uses them, on what enigmatical errands? The steps on Rock Street, flanked with ivy, giving on a deserted, grass-grown lot—who owns them? Who climbs up to stand among the forlorn trees, looking down on the railroad track? Do these steps serve any practical purpose, or are they placed here just to make us wonder?

Gates

THE WORD *pedestrian* has two meanings. One is neutral, describing things involving walking, including people who go on foot. The other meaning has a negative connotation: commonplace or unimaginative. This implies a slur against walking, the oldest, cheapest, and most basic form of transportation. Viewed together on the page of a dictionary, the two definitions give off a faint air of disapproval: Don't be so pedestrian! Upgrade to something smarter! Are you still using feet?

I can agree that walking is commonplace, but never that it is unimaginative. Only walk to the top of Hillside Avenue—not the one in the Park View neighborhood but the other Hillside Avenue, near Purcell Park (in the undulant Friendly City, it's almost surprising that only two streets claim this name). Do not be alarmed by the Dead End sign. It's not for you. Pass with confidence between the unassuming houses, their featureless lawns and untenanted wooden porches, and the trees, almost leafless at this season, that extend their branches against a porcelain sky. You are approaching the top of the hill. A fence appears, blocking the street. At this point, you may feel a shade of doubt. Is this a dead end after all? Will you have to turn and retrace your steps, glancing about to see if a face is watching you mockingly from a window, burying your chin in your collar and pretending to be in a hurry, in the sheepish manner of people who have gone the wrong way?

Fear not! Look to your right, and you'll see a little open gate, charmingly overgrown like the entrance to a garden. It leads you onto the bike path, which traverses a huge, bare parking lot on its way down to the university. From the half-hidden, woodsy gate, so delicious to slip through, like something out of a fairy tale, you are tossed out onto a tarmac expanse with a science-fictional atmosphere, like a landing strip for spacecraft.

Walking stimulates the imagination. Passing through a gate tucked away in some corner of the city, moving from one type of terrain to another, I feel my thoughts turn unexpected corners. I recommend to you our cemetery gates: the gates of the Jewish cemetery, which you open by pulling out a fantastic old-fashioned iron spike, and the red-painted gates of Woodbine, especially the modest one on Bruce Street, scarcely noticeable behind the headstones, which seems to have been left ajar by a ghostly hand.

Routes

I HAVE SUNG the alleys of our city, the intimate backstreets peppered with gravel or grassy like long green ribbons behind the houses, tunneling between the sheds and gardens, inconvenient for wheeled traffic but delightful for walkers, a gift designed just for us. These routes form a precious network across the city. But I would like to mention another wonderful path, perhaps not as widely known—one that leads out of the city. I have often left my house on foot, carrying my backpack, and headed off to dine in the shadow of the Empire State Building.

Perhaps it's not quite fair to include this route in my notes on walking, since it involves a bus and a train. But I can't resist divulging this marvelous pedestrian secret. Yes, you can go to dinner in the Big Apple from the Friendly City on your own two feet! Or, if you prefer, you can enjoy a late lunch in the capital!

I step out onto my porch at around ten o'clock in the morning, pack on my back and tote bag over my shoulder, pulling a rolling suitcase if I'm planning a longish stay. I walk through town to the state university campus. There I walk up the steps of a bus that carries me out of the city, through a landscape of purplish, tumbled mountains, the clouds lying over them in clear layers, the words "Endless Caverns" picked out in white against the ridge. We arrive at the capital city. I walk down to the lower level of the station and board a train. Scenes flit by in the window: crumbling townhouses, factories, rivers. At six in the evening, I am walking through the wide, crowded streets of the metropolis to the Italian restaurant where I have planned to meet a friend.

I sit down to wait, perusing the menu, my bags stowed under the table, my legs tingling from the day's exercise, my whole body filled with the elation of having accomplished this journey so smoothly, with so little stress, in this happy, pedestrian way. The fading light of dusk falls through the window, mingled with the rays of the streetlamps. It gilds the silk rose on the table and touches the edge of my shoe—this sturdy, well-worn Friendly City shoe, which so recently crossed my porch. And I am amazed to think of the places I can go, and the distances I can travel, simply by walking out my front door.

December

Non-Places

ADMITTEDLY, it was an odd decision to walk to the mall. Malls were not made to fit a walker's routine. These massive, enclosed shopping centers arose in the 1950s, part of a shift that included the growth of the suburbs and automobile culture. Malls are often blamed for the decay of American city centers, because their superstores and movie theaters drew people away from local downtown venues, encouraging residents to discard a walk to the corner store in favor of a drive to the mall.

My walk to the mall takes me down Evelyn Byrd Avenue to University Boulevard, where I'm stranded without a sidewalk, a sure sign that the needs of pedestrians have been left out of this urban plan. Feeling a bit like an unwanted pest—some random rodent calculating its best chances of survival in a world of asphalt—I scramble up a slope covered with wood chips toward the comparative safety of a parking lot. The day is cold and bright, the sky a gulf of wintry blue. The vast, pale-amber citadel of the mall rises against the ridge, and I make my way toward it with the awkward, clownish maneuvers of a walker in an area designed for cars, jumping down curbs, dashing across driveways, and barging between the shrubs of landscaped barriers.

In his 1992 book, written during the heyday of shopping

malls, the anthropologist Marc Augé analyzes what he calls "non-places": modern forms like highways, department stores, and airport lounges that defy the usual methods of anthropology. Traditionally, Augé observes, anthropologists study small, distinctive spaces: villages and rural communities with dense layers of history and culture. How should an anthropologist take on an anonymous space like this parking lot I'm hurrying through, ducking my head against the wind, or the bland, windowless edifice of the mall, decked with signs for big stores and company logos, that might be part of any landscape, anywhere?

According to Augé, an anthropologist of non-places must address the world created there, which is solitary and contractual. These are zones of transit rather than dwelling, of retail rather than social exchange, of convenience rather than experience. Identity is flattened; in a mall we are all the same, listening to the same background music, guided by the same instructions ("No Smoking," "Place your items in the bagging area"). Entering the mall, with its self-effacing gray floor tiles and understated, anodyne lighting, I'm reminded of childhood, of passing through the doors of another mall, which, though belonging to a different place and time, was very much like this one, inducing the same feeling—pallid, insipid, and vaguely stifling—of stepping into a giant marshmallow.

It's strange that our landscape is arranged to discourage walking to the mall, since once you get there, all you do is walk. Up and down the halls I go, passing the lighted windows, the shoe displays, the mannikins gazing into the distance. I remember that on days like this, when the temperature dropped toward freezing, my father used to drive to our local mall to walk for exercise, circling the place in his sneakers along with many other middle-aged people for whom this seemed to be a trend at the time. Originally, the word *mall* meant a public place for walking. Victor Gruen, the architect of the postwar mall, envisioned a utopian, pedestrian-friendly space, with housing, schools, and parks as well as shops. When he visited the malls that were actually built from his designs—chunks of stores surrounded by what he called "the ugliness and discomfort of the land-wasting seas of parking"—he was horrified. His imagined place had become a non-place. One of the only bits of his dream to survive, I reflect as I wander through the "gigantic shopping machine" he deplored, is the act of walking.

I'm with Victor Gruen: I don't love malls. Roaming these colorless corridors, I feel like an old-fashioned anthropologist, desperate for signs of novel human activity, gasping for something that isn't standardized. But malls are embedded in culture and influence our collective fantasy life. They form the backdrop of beloved films and TV shows, many of them with a Christmas theme, I recall as I pass beneath the gargantuan tree with its regular pattern of fake snow and dim bronze balls. For Augé, non-places create "neither singular identity nor relations; only solitude and similitude." But isn't there an emotional link between the mall and the holiday season, something that exceeds monetary transactions and becomes a cultural mood? Isn't nostalgia relational? I think of an online conversation I read recently, full of reminiscences about the Friendly City, in which people enthuse over the old mall, the food court, and the candy store. For one contributor, the uniformity of malls across the country is a comforting reminder of the past. "Yes," another exclaims, "I love that every mall feels the same! I think it's the smell."

It's strange, too, that a mall should be haunting. One would expect a non-place to be too sterile and devoid of human interest to raise a ghost. But there's an unmistakable melancholy to the mall, a tinge of abandonment and encroaching decay. Under a series of misfortunes—economic recession, the rise of online shopping, the pandemic—American malls have begun to collapse, many shutting down altogether in what some have called a retail apocalypse. Our mall shows signs of this general decline. Closed stores with dark, gridded windows exude a mournful air. Instead of a variety of ads for different products, one sees a repeated sign: Leasing Now. "Get creative," beg the posters on the deserted booths down the center of the walkway, with a poignant attempt at positive thinking. "We have the space."

And the cardboard figures standing outside one of the shuttered businesses, portraying a larger-than-life gingerbread village—how sad they are, in their gaudy colors, beaming good cheer toward the empty hall, the roundheaded children smiling gamely beside their king-size dog! Surely these decorations express the essence of the mall: extravagantly big, with a cookie-cutter lack of individuality, associated with childhood and the explosive consumerism of the American holiday season, looking sweet enough to make your mouth water, but finally inedible, and shadowed by the gloom of a dead store. Then again, considering some of the proposed plans and current projects to repurpose fading American malls, transforming them into mixed-use neighborhoods from the visions of Victor Gruen, it's just possible that this faux-gingerbread town foreshadows, like an image in a dream, the next life of this non-place: a future place where the sun will shine, fresh air will blow, real kids will play, and living people will walk their warm and breathing dogs.

Street Haunting

"How beautiful a street is in winter!" wrote Virginia Woolf. "It is at once revealed and obscured." She wrote in the great city of London, where she had gone out on a winter's evening to buy a pencil; we write in the little Friendly City, where we are going to the co-op to buy some chocolate-covered almonds for a party.

At once the comparison feels presumptuous. We are not Virginia Woolf, and the Friendly City, when called upon to stand in for the foreign metropolis, shivers from Park View to Sentara, ducks its head in an agony of bashfulness, and threatens to gather up its streets and retreat from view. But as we set out on a December afternoon, wrapped up against the chill that has settled down over the rooftops, we find that our city, like that of another writer in another country almost a hundred years ago, is revealed and obscured, exposed by the leafless branches and dimmed by the cloudy sky.

There is something inspiring about the first breath of cold. We had almost forgotten that our valley could produce this weather. The buffeting wind calls up a spirit of adventure, rousing us to prolong our walk, to stride up Elizabeth Street and see how the old houses look in the slant of the winter light, to climb as high as we can, up to the very edge of the city, where a line of pine trees borders the cemetery. Here we can gaze down over the town, which appears to be half sky. A white sheet of cloud conceals most of this sky, like a blind in a window; beneath it, a band of airy blue borders the deeper blue of the mountains; under the mountains lie the sloping streets of the town.

Reflecting on Virginia Woolf's essay about haunting the streets of London, we recall that while she writes wonderfully about houses, shops, and people, there is very little in her record about the sky. But in the Friendly City, the sky is always one's companion. At times it shrinks, when one descends into a gap between hills, but it's always ready to spring up again, expanding, when one reaches the top of some elevation, into a slowly whirling spectacle of color. Even now the sky is changing. The wall of mist breaks up and darkens; separate clouds take shape, almost black in the center but ringed with silver; milky folds sink down against the mountains, so thick the light can only come through sluggishly, giving them a faint gloss like the sheen on marble. At this height, we belong to the sky more than the city, which looks like a toy town, the streets laid out under our eye as if on a living-room carpet, lined with miniature houses, furnished with a wee grain elevator, and topped with the steeple of a baby church.

We wonder if it will ever be possible to feel immersed in the Friendly City, plunged into a teeming urban mass. Even if the city sprawls to enormous proportions, it will keep these hills. Will it always have this aspect of a toy town, then? Will it always feel, in some way, small?

As we walk back downhill, the mountains shed their

mulberry glow over the weatherbeaten houses, the run-down cars, the unkempt yards full of children's bicycles flung down at random, basketballs, rakes, discarded furniture, and forgotten shoes. Dogs bark wildly behind the walls. There's a palpable sense of life—jumpy, haphazard, vulnerable—going on all over the street. How amazing it is to find so much vibrant disorder at this height, against such a view! In many places, such vistas belong only to the rich. Hotels command them; pristine, soundproof condominiums claim the most beautiful situations. But here, school buses still trundle up and down the steep incline, and children disembark, squabbling and waving the crumpled paper snowflakes they made at school, which will be pasted up in the dusty windows that look out on the blue flanks of the mountains and the inexhaustible glory of the sky. Ordinary people enjoy this vision every day. As we pass a sagging house whose steps have been propped up here and there with bricks, a diminutive elderly man emerges with a colossal dog that, startled by our presence, goes for us with a vehement howl. The old man just manages to restrain his companion. For a long time, as we continue down the sidewalk, we can hear him cursing in a squeaky voice while the animal, still barking ferociously, bounds all over the place, dragging him behind it. We can't help smiling. In the deepening twilight, lamplit windows have begun peeping through the overgrown shrubbery, and strings of holiday lights twinkle along the porches. Dear little street, may you always stay this way, untrimmed and flickering, with your loose boards, rowdy children, and uncouth pets!

Here is the co-op, warm and bright. The chocolate-covered almonds, shiny as beads, tumble into our paper bag. Here is our own street, mantled with clouds, where golden garlands of festive lights cluster, winking in the wind. We remember beginning our notes on the Friendly City, almost a year ago. It was winter then, too, and the streets were revealed and obscured, like now, and thinking of this, we realize how both walking and writing depend on the habit of attention, whether in a large city or a small one. A street can't be revealed in an abstract sense; it can only be revealed *to* someone. Revelation implies relationship. Somebody has to notice. And the strange thing about the habit of attention is that it transforms the looker internally, as if the act of seeing works on the unseen part of oneself.

Big town or small town, mountains or flatland, boulevard or sky? In the end, a concentrated focus on perception divulges a secret: The things seen are less important than the seeing eye. Having haunted the streets of the Friendly City so faithfully during these months, we feel capable of haunting any street in the world.

Salvage

IMAGINE YOUR TOWN was not going to last forever. If it was to be changed beyond recognition, what would you wish to salvage from the remains? If you had to leave, what would you want to take with you?

The streets with their elemental names: Rock, Water, Hill.

Ice in the gutters, blinding.

Light picking out the snow on the bushes and cars. The streets are black; the dust of snow will melt away by noon. Watching, I try not to breathe, not to break this brief spell of winter.

Clouds in patches, bluish, smoky, ivory, like uneven, swirling blots of paint, each scuffed at the edges as if the brush, lifting from the canvas, has left behind a faint imprint of horsehair.

The changing seasons. Kids fishing in the pond at Purcell Park.

Cornflowers in the cracks of the curb. Graffiti on a bridge: "Homesick."

Strolling by a window, looking straight through the house to the mountains beyond, thinking of the poet John Casteen: "my Blue Ridge, collapsing into creamy hayfields."

Walking through the cemetery, like a metaphor of passing through life, and the beautiful blooming dogwood standing pink among the graves, and the wind, soft, humid, neutral, neither too warm nor too cool: the temperature of human skin.

The deep-green summer grass, the deep-green trees, the blue-gray sky that follows several days of rain with more to come.

Complete cloud cover. The low house on the corner under big overarching trees. A collection of cracked, threadbare porch furniture.

A stone statue of a nymph against the darkness of an open garage door, surrounded by nodding, peach-colored roses.

Serene full moon in a dark blue sky, sending out four delicate streams of ghostly light in the shape of a cross. Not a breath of wind. Sinking behind the rooftops, the moon looks yellower, cut by telephone wires. And when it slides behind a pole, the air having changed from a blue darkness to a blue light that shows up the shabbiness of the house across the street, the silent contented shut-eyed somehow perfect shabbiness of that peeling house, as serene as the moon itself—then you can tell that the moon, golden now and without its ghostly cross, pure yellow gold like a coin, is not sinking straight down but sailing in a gentle arc across the sky.

An evening in late July. Fireflies wink from the Queen Anne's lace along the road.

Three motionless rabbits, turned sideways, watching me—small, young rabbits under the streetlamp.

Parchment-colored rocks in the dry creek bed at Hillendale Park.

The moment before a storm. The crackling air: like breathing cinders.

The houses painted in striking colors—aqua, purple, pink. A bright orange door. A feeling of amateur art. (In a local paper from 1924, the jubilant capital letters: "We Do Not Know of Another Community in the South Where So Many Homes Are Painted.")

Rocking chairs on a porch. A china dog with its head on its paws.

The humped, alien outline of a tree branch wrapped in cobwebs—great skeins of thread encasing the leaves like a tissue.

A strange night sky, almost completely white. Looking north up the street, it's dark, but to the south it's all white, as if the clouds are somehow lighting up the sky, which glows blue between them—dark blue, but still blue. Streetlights? Factory? Moon? Why is it so light out?

Rose of Sharon. Flowering gourd.

The black maple. Its brooding maroon.

A little white church at the bottom of a hill.

The sleepy morning streets. No sound except when a school bus passes.

Tin roofs. Scarlet flash of a cardinal's wing.

In the post-rain, pre-rain sky, a line of cloud all along the mountains, stroked back by the wind like combed fleece. The whiteness diffuses into spots, drawn up into the murk above the peaks, the mountains to the left sinking down into a sea of white wool, while on the right Massanutten stands up sharp, prominent, and dark, surrounded by a glistening ruff like the rings of Saturn.

Weekend parties for Labor Day. Cars parked on the grass.

A patterned window like the segments of an orange.

Rumor of an escaped goat on my street. All the kids out looking for the goat that got away from the livestock auction. There is already a neighborhood plan: Someone's sister-in-law has a farm in the country. The goat will be captured and smuggled to safety.

Interiors. A colored lampshade in a window. Books.

A calm, greenish sky, almost turquoise, and the dainty clouds stitched on with a little floss, a color I can't isolate—I imagine it as white, but I think it's really more of a light gray (all the missed opportunities for photographs).

Mullioned windows. Ivy.

People playing music on a porch: guitar, fiddle, banjo, bass.

A crisp wind sweeping away the stink of the factory.

The railroad track pursuing its mysterious way through town, receding into the distance, going *there*.

Snow again: a few flakes. A damp white sky, the mountains hidden behind the haze, and the veiled trees like charcoal smudges.

Hiss of the sleet in magnolia leaves.

The street, slick with moisture, reflecting the gleam of the living-room window. Porch light. Home.

The Romance of Closeness

THE YEAR IS ENDING, and I'm walking uphill again. I cross the square under a low, cloudy sky and hike up Green Street, then turn onto Chicago Avenue, thinking that it's the last time I will write these weekly notes, remembering why I started. There were several reasons. I'd never written to deadlines before, and I thought the obligation would provide an interesting discipline. I love walking in the Friendly City, and I felt that people should know what a wonderful place this is to walk, as well as the times when it's not so wonderful (disappearing sidewalks, truncated paths). I wanted to share this experience in all its random, quirky, astonishing ordinariness. To uncover the marvelous in the everyday. To trace the seasons, exploring the shifts in weather throughout the year. To capture, if I could, the texture of a place.

A collection of furniture stands in a yard; someone must be moving. The mirror of a bureau reflects the sky, this stern winter sky in which the clouds have thickened, while a ray of white sunlight pierces the gloom, flooding the housefronts. Only in winter, I think, is the sky at once so dark and so bright. I have to turn away from the mirror in the yard when it catches the dazzling sun. The effect feels almost deliberate, as if this sidewalk jumble is an art installation, and I think of one of my inspirations for these essays, the surrealist writer

Louis Aragon, whose book *Paris Peasant*, written a hundred years ago, records his ecstatic experiences of urban wandering. I share Aragon's desire for a sense of enchantment with common scenes. Like him, I want to cultivate a heightened awareness that can draw the force of myth from familiar objects. There's an intense kind of noticing, at which Aragon excelled, that reveals one's surroundings as a fathomless reservoir of strangeness and delight.

Walking up Greystone Street, I observe another artwork, an intentional one this time, the type of surrealist tableau our city provides regularly, free of charge, for the entertainment of passersby: a fantastical display of lawn ornaments. Two smartly dressed foxes, seated on a bench, enjoy a picnic lunch. A little dog peers into a birdbath. Minnie Mouse lurks behind a tree. A patient donkey stands hitched to a cart that bears a cascade of living foliage. A happy chaos reigns among these figures, as in dreams; realistic portrayals and relations are abandoned; the white doves kissing above a garland of roses are bigger than the foxes, while Minnie Mouse looms over a chipped blue squirrel. Temporal order is no more respected than spatial proportion: Popular and classical images blend in this peaceable kingdom, where a stone merchild with the blank eyes of Greek statuary plays a conch for an audience of two cows, a bonneted Victorian doll, and a brontosaurus.

When I began to write about walking, I wanted to record the charm of these things, both the small ones and the large: the planter shaped like a boot on Smith Avenue, the houses built up on the hillside with their balconies overlooking the town, and the mountains, always the mountains, now aglow beneath lifting clouds, the shadows on their flanks electric blue. I hoped to develop the sensibility of a poet, as described by Ralph Waldo Emerson, another model of the walking writer. "The poet's habit of living," Emerson wrote, "should be set on a key so low that the common influences should delight him. His cheerfulness should be the gift of the sunlight; the air should suffice for his inspiration, and he should be tipsy with water."

To be like Emerson's poet, thrilled with little things. A Christmas wreath. A dead-end street giving onto a secret path where a walker can slip through. Crossing the road, I think of the writer Lydia Davis, whose conversation with her friend, the Norwegian writer Johanne Fronth-Nygren, inspired both this writing project and a change in my life. These two writers discussed their decision to stop flying as part of a response to the climate crisis. I was struck by their candid reflections on what they were losing by making this choice, but also by their sense of gain and discovery. For Davis, deciding not to fly "results in a greater concentration on the local, on valuing what is here. Once I am not expecting more and more, looking outward farther and farther, a circle is drawn around what I have, but within that circle there is more attention, I look deeper inside the circle, and what remains has greater value." I've traveled a great deal in my life, and trips to distant places have often energized my writing, so for me the decision to reduce air travel meant reinventing myself as a writer, envisioning a new approach to both art and life. Writing this column was part of my attempt to look, as Davis puts it, "deeper inside the circle," to recognize and value what is here.

A hedge of winterberry holly sparkles along the wall of a church, the scarlet berries like jewels in a brittle brown net. A clump of silver grass turns incandescent in the sun, going up like a struck match in tufts of whitish flame. The habit of attention has proved more powerful than I expected; I don't think I've fully understood its influence yet. I only know how lovely the city is in every season. I think of the writer Robert Walser, yet another source of inspiration, and a character in his novel *The Tanners*, who remarks that the trees don't travel, so why should he? The trees change without moving. "When I find myself in a city in winter, I feel tempted to see it in spring," this character explains. "Seeing a tree in winter I wish to see it resplendent in the springtime, sending out its first enchanting leaves."

Seeing these trees in winter, I want to see them in the spring. I feel I will never exhaust this little city. How much I failed to record during this year of writing—how many scenes, corners, curiosities, and dramas of weather and light! "However closely we approach the everyday," wrote Aragon, "it can never be close enough." I wrote every week, but I wanted to say this every minute: that the blue of the sky behind the neighbor's roof was darker than usual this morning; that the creek ran high and clear; that the mountains slumbered under layers of cloud, blurred and feathery, rubbing out the line between earth and heaven; that the streets were wrapped in silence, but the café on the square already glittered, busy with steam and cheerful talk; that this was our town, and we loved it; that this was our time, and we lived it; that we were here, just here, and we were alive.

Acknowledgments

Many thanks to Andrew Jenner, Bridget Manley, and the team at *The Harrisonburg Citizen* for providing a space for this project.

For your guidance and expertise, thanks to Brent Finnegan, Kayla Grose, and Charlie Wingard.

For editing and shaping this collection into a book, thanks to Keith Miller.

For your conversation, suggestions, and enthusiasm, thanks to Erica Cavanagh, Debbie Glick Phillips, David J. Gonzol, Hadley Jenner, Tim Jost, Keith A. May, Harold F. Miller, Phyllis Ressler, Mark Sawin, Mary Ann Zehr, and all the first readers of my column.

Archive

Aragon, Louis. *Paris Peasant*. Translated by Simon Watson Taylor. Exact Change, 2011.

@Shoottheradio. "Let's reminisce about older H-Burg." Reddit. Archived post, accessed December 4, 2024. https://www.reddit.com/r/harrisonburg/comments/17jtyso/.lets_reminisce_about_older_hburg/.

Augé, Marc. *Non-Places: Introduction to an Anthropology of Supermodernity*. Translated by John Howe. Verso, 1995.

Benjamin, Walter. *Illuminations*. Translated by Harry Zohn. Schocken Books, 1968.

Benjamin, Walter. *Moscow Diary*. Translated by Richard Sieburth. Harvard University Press, 1986.

Benjamin, Walter. *Selected Writings, Volume I: 1913–1926*. Edited by Marcus Bullock and Michael W. Jennings. Harvard University Press, 1996.

Bell, Byrdie (@byrdiebell). "Paying a visit to the famed and friendly ghost of the first Evelyn Byrd back at Westover Plantation." Instagram, October 12, 2023. https://www.instagram.com/p/CyTMIRiOOcx/.

Bettelheim, Bruno. *The Uses of Enchantment: The Meaning and Importance of Fairy Tales*. Vintage Books, 2010.

"Blacks Run Clean Up Day." Clean Stream. Accessed March 6, 2024. https://www.harrisonburgva.gov/cleanstream-get-involved#BlacksRunCleanUpDay.

Boros, Chris, and Pat Jarrett. "Episode Eleven: Rocky McIntire & DIY Virginia Punk Houses." Folklife Fieldnotes. *WMRA*, January 26, 2023.

Carson, Anne. *Plainwater: Essays and Poetry*. Vintage Books, 1995.

Casteen, John. *Free Union*. University of Georgia Press, 2009.

"Celebrating Simms Collection." *Celebrating Simms: The Story of the Lucy F. Simms School*. Accessed March 27, 2024. https://omeka.lib.jmu.edu/simms/collections/show/8.

"Charles Keck." Wikipedia. Accessed July 24, 2024. https://en.wikipedia.org/wiki/Charles_Keck.

Curl, John, ed. and trans. *Ancient American Poets*. Bilingual Press, 2005.

Daily News-Record (Harrisonburg, VA). Jan. 12, 1924.

"Dallard-Newman House." Roots Run Deep. Accessed March 27, 2024. https://rootsrundeep.org/dallard-newman-house.html.

Davis, Lydia, and Johanne Fronth-Nygren. "Lydia Davis on Making the Decision Not to Fly." *Literary Hub*, July 20, 2020. https://lithub.com/lydia-davis-on-making-the-decision-not-to-fly/.

"Desire Path." Wikipedia. Accessed September 25, 2024. https://en.wikipedia.org/wiki/Desire_path.

Dillard, Annie. *Pilgrim at Tinker Creek*. Harper Perennial, 2007.

Du Bois, W. E. B. *The Souls of Black Folk*. W. W. Norton, 2022.

"East Campus Hillside." James Madison University Institute for Stewardship of the Natural World. Accessed April 17, 2024. https://www.jmu.edu/stewardship/tour/hillside.shtml.

Ehrenpreis, David. *Picturing Harrisonburg: Visions of a Shenandoah Valley City Since 1828*. University of Virginia Press, 2017.

Emerson, Ralph Waldo. *Ralph Waldo Emerson: Essential Essays*. Warbler Press, 2023.

"Evelyn Byrd." Historic Westover. Accessed October 30, 2024. https://historicwestover.com/evelyn-byrd.htm.

Fénéon, Félix. *Novels in Three Lines*. Translated by Luc Sante. New York Review Books, 2005.

García Lorca, Federico. *A Season in Granada: Uncollected Poems and Prose*. Translated by Christopher Maurer. Anvil Press, 1998.

Gladwell, Malcom. "The Terrestrial Jungle." *The New Yorker*, March 7, 2004.

Glissant, Édouard. *Poetics of Relation*. Translated by Betsy Wing. University of Michigan Press, 1997.

Greenaway, Kate. *The Language of Flowers*. Frederick Warne, 1977.

Grundmann, Mike. "With State Grant Funding, HPD Provides Increased Security for City's Jewish and Muslim Congregations." *The Harrisonburg Citizen*, June 20, 2024. https://hburgcitizen.com/2024/06/20/with-state-grant-funding-hpd-provides-increased-security-for-citys-jewish-muslim-congregations/.

Gumbel, Andrew. "How Giant Stores Changed the Face of America." *The Independent*, November 1, 2007. https://www.independent.co.uk/news/world/americas/how-giant-stores-changed-face-of-america-398464.html.

Hagi, Randi B. "Long-Polluted Blacks Run Is Making a Comeback. Ducks and Fish Love It. Now a New Program Can Spur Residents to Help." *The Harrisonburg Citizen*, June 21, 2019. https://hburgcitizen.com/2019/06/21/long-polluted-blacks-run-is-making-a-comeback-ducks-and-fish-love-it-now-a-new-program-can-spur-residents-to-help/.

Hagi, Randi B. "The Legacy of Harrisonburg's 'Urban Renewal.'" *WMRA*, February 11, 2020. https://www.wmra.org/wmra-news/2020-02-11/the-legacy-of-harrisonburgs-urban-renewal.

"History." Northeast Neighborhood Association. Accessed February 17, 2025. https://web.archive.org/web/20231114134852/https://www.nenava.org/history.html.

Hopkins, Gerard Manley. *Gerard Manley Hopkins: Selected Poetry*. Oxford University Press, 1996.

Johnson, Colby. "Mennonite Action Begins 11-Day March to Washington D.C. to Call for Ceasefire in Gaza." *WHSV3*, July 18, 2024. https://www.whsv.com/2024/07/18/mennonite-action-begins-11-day-march-washington-dc-call-ceasefire-gaza/.

Kracauer, Siegfried. "Memory of a Paris Street." Translated by Ross Benjamin. *Words Without Borders*, September 1, 2009. https://wordswithoutborders.org/read/article/2009-09/memory-of-a-paris-street/.

Lee, Marguerite duPont. *Virginia Ghosts*. Virginia Book Company, 1966.

Lewis, C. S. *The Magician's Nephew*. The Bodley Head, 1955.

Li, Qing. *Forest Bathing: How Trees Can Help You Find Health and Happiness*. Penguin Life, 2018.

Lucretius, Titus Carus. *On the Nature of Things*. Translated by W. H. D. Rouse. Harvard University Press, 1924.

Lüthi, Max. *Once Upon a Time: On the Nature of Fairy Tales*. Translated by Lee Chadeayne and Paul Gottwald. F. Ungar, 1970.

Lynch, Kevin. *The Image of the City*. The MIT Press, 1960.

Manley, Bridget. "The Future Is as Murky as the Past for the House That Wasn't Thomas Harrison's." *The Harrisonburg Citizen*, October 8, 2021. https://hburgcitizen.com/2021/10/08/the-future-is-as-murky-as-the-past-for-the-house-that-wasnt-thomas-harrisons/.

Marks, Laura U. *Enfoldment and Infinity: An Islamic Genealogy of New Media Art*. The MIT Press, 2010.

Missing Middle Housing. Accessed July 17, 2024. https://missingmiddlehousing.com/.

Moser, Benjamin. *Why This World: A Biography of Clarice Lispector*. Oxford University Press, 2009.

Mullen, Harryette. *Urban Tumbleweed: Notes from a Tanka Diary*. Graywolf Press, 2013.

Myers, David. "Belmar: 'Urbanizing' a Suburban Colorado Mall." *Urban Land*, July 25, 2013.

Newman, George. *A Miserable Revenge: A Story of Life in Virginia*. Edited by Mollie Godfrey, Brooks E. Hefner, Jeslyn Pool, and Evan Sizemore. James Madison University Libraries, 2025.

"Northend Greenway." City of Harrisonburg Public Works. Accessed March 13, 2024. https://www.harrisonburgva.gov/northend-greenway.

Novalis. *Philosophical Writings*. Translated by Margaret Mahony Stoljar. State University of New York, 1997.

Perec, Georges. *An Attempt at Exhausting a Place in Paris*. Translated by Marc Lowenthal. Wakefield Press, 2010.

Proust, Marcel. *Pleasures and Days*. Translated by Andrew Brown. Alma Classics, 2013.

"Purcell Park Collection." Rocktown History. Accessed May 1, 2024. https://valleyheritagemuseum.pastperfectonline.com/archive/01495CC5-632F-4895-9D61-280231994870.

Ray, Jean. "The Shadowy Street." In *The Weird: A Compendium of Strange and Dark Stories*, edited by Ann VanderMeer and Jeff VanderMeer. Tor Books, 2011.

"Rockingham County Courthouse." SAH Archipedia. Accessed March 6, 2024. https://sah-archipedia.org/buildings/VA-02-RH1.

"Rockingham County World War I Memorial." The Historical Marker Database. Accessed July 24, 2024. https://www.hmdb.org/m.asp?m=263585.

Sachdev, Shaan. "Baudelaire Would Be Run Over in New York City Today." *The New York Times*, Jan. 7, 2024.

Stepler, Kellen. "Effort to Restore 'Lady Liberty' Begins." *The Daily News-Record*, February 5, 2022. Updated March 11, 2024. https://www.dnronline.com/dnronline/effort-to-restore-lady-liberty-begins/article_551b2a27-2f5f-5396-993c-7cfa7bef7edb.html.

Suter, Scott Hamilton. *Shenandoah Valley Folklife*. University Press of Mississippi, 1999.

Taylor, L. B. Jr. *The Ghosts of Virginia*. Progress Printing, 1995.

Tolkien, J. R. R. *The Lord of the Rings*. HarperCollins Publishers, 1991.

Tolkien, J. R. R. *Tolkien on Fairy Stories*. HarperCollins Publishers, 2014.

Tomes, Hannah. "The Twists and Turns of 'Desire Paths.'" *The Spectator*, July 9, 2022. https://www.spectator.co.uk/article/the-twists-and-turns-of-desire-paths/.

"Tree Campus USA." James Madison University Facilities Management. Accessed April 17, 2024, https://www.jmu.edu/facmgt/sustainability/tree-campus/index.shtml.

Walser, Robert. *The Tanners*. Translated by Susan Bernofsky. New Directions, 2010.

"We Finally Figured Out Why It Smells Like Dog Food." *The Tab*, February 1, 2016. https://archive.thetab.com/us/jmu/2016/02/01/dog-food-smell-405#:~:text=Harrisonburg%20is%20in%20fact%20famous,especially%20strong%20in%20wet%20weather.

Whitlock, Rosemary. *The Monacan Indian Nation of Virginia: The Drums of Life*. University of Alabama Press, 2008.

Williams, William Carlos. *Paterson*. New Directions, 1995.

Woolf, Virginia. *The Death of the Moth and Other Essays*. Harcourt, Brace, Jovanovich, 1974.

About the Author

SOFIA SAMATAR is a writer of fiction and nonfiction, including the memoir *The White Mosque*, a PEN/Jean Stein Award finalist. Her works range from the World Fantasy Award–winning novel *A Stranger in Olondria* to *Opacities: On Writing and the Writing Life*, a National Book Critics Circle Award Longlist selection. She lives in Harrisonburg, Virginia, and teaches at James Madison University.

www.ingramcontent.com/pod-product-compliance
Lightning Source LLC
Chambersburg PA
CBHW060556080526
44585CB00013B/580